Hill Country Cookin' and Memoirs

Grandmama and Grandpapa Lane and Aunt Ibbie.

Hill Country Cookin' and Memoirs

Ibbie Ledford

Pelican Publishing Company
Gretna 1991

Library of Congress Cataloging-in-Publication Data

Ledford, Ibbie.
    Hill country cookin' and memoirs / by Ibbie Ledford.
      p. cm.
    Includes index.
    ISBN 0-88289-848-5
    1. Cookery, American—Southern style. 2. Cookery—
Tennessee. 3. Tennessee—Social life and customs. I. Title. II.
Title: Hill country cooking and memoirs.
TX715.2.S68L44 1991
641.59768—dc20   91-12217
                                     CIP

Manufactured in the United States of America
Published by Pelican Publishing Company, Inc.
1101 Monroe Street, Gretna, Louisiana 70053

To Willie, my first, last, and only husband. To our children, Debby, Steve, and Tim, and to our grandchildren. You are the loves of my life.

To my dear friend Maxine Buchwald. Without your faith and encouragement, Mickey, I would never have been able to write this book.

To Dude, who asked why I wanted to write a book when I could go to the store and buy one for three dollars.

And to Mama and Papa. Since I'm the ninth child, I ask you, "Am I lucky or what?" I'd say lucky there were no birth control pills at the time I was conceived. I know Mama was never sorry she had any of us after we arrived. She was that kind of mother. If given a choice, however, very few women would choose to have ten children. Thanks, Mom. I'm aware of the many sacrifices you and Papa made to raise us.

Someone once said to Mama, "At your age [she was ninety-one at the time] how do you stand so straight?" Mama replied, "I stand straight and proud because I'm so proud of my children. They all look like movie stars, and there's not a rotten apple in the bunch." When my sister, Johnnie, began to mention some unattractive movie stars as our look-alikes, Mama became very aggravated, for you see she was thinking of the beautiful people. Poor Mama was not only blinded by glaucoma, but was always blinded by love.

Thanks, Mom. Thanks, Papa. Thanks for life, your love, and thanks for the memories.

A scene near our home.

Contents

My friend Donna and me holding chickens.

Introduction

It has been said, "The heart of a home is the kitchen." Like me, many women spend much of their lives in this one room preparing meals for their families. Since cooking has been a very enjoyable part of my life, I thought it time to put my recipe collection together in book form. Many of the recipes in this book are my own originals; some are from Mama's collection; others have been acquired through the years from friends and other family members. Many are of a regional, Southern hill country flavor, as are the short stories. They are simple, stick-to-the-rib recipes using ingredients that are readily available at the nearest grocery store. Most are flexible enough to allow one to take away, add, or adjust ingredients to one's own taste.

The book depicts a life-style I knew as a child growing up on a farm with nine brothers and sisters, a life-style that will never be again. I was born in 1932 in the middle of the Great Depression. Big families were common in those days. Mama and Papa had ten children—six boys and four girls. I was the ninth child and Papa's baby girl. We raised some of everything on the farm, canning and storing summer's bounty to feed ourselves and the animals until time to harvest another crop. Farming was hard work and everyone did their share. Even the smallest child could tote in stove wood, feed chickens, and gather the eggs.

We had very little materially, but we were happy kids. I guess we were poor, but I didn't feel poor. I didn't even know we were poor. Life was simpler then and the rewards greater appreciated. Families were close: my two best friends were cousins. My stories are of a time when your work was your bond, a handshake was a deal, and neighbors could be counted on in any emergency or difficult situation.

The story on porch sitting recalls a very enjoyable pastime in my childhood. One story, "Preaching All Day and Dinner on the Grounds," accompanied by the recipe for Scripture Cake, tells of the event of the year for our little community, when families and friends gathered at the church house to share food for the body and food for the soul. Other stories of the times are, "The Lights," "The Sanitary Toilet," and "Designer Originals."

Memories know no boundaries, reaching across the years and across many miles. They can be pleasant, causing us to smile; or unpleasant, causing withdrawal and many problems of the mind. I have very few sad or tragic memories. Most are of a pleasant nature and, when recalled, bring a smile or a tug on the heartstrings. These memories and recipes of a long ago time—so different from the now times of our children and grandchildren—I will share with you in this book.

Appetizers and Snacks

Aunt Ibbie, Uncle Willie, and Aunt Ibbie's T Model.

ALMOND CHICKEN BALLS

1 pkg. (8 oz.) cream cheese
1 cup chopped cooked chicken
1 cup herb-seasoned stuffing mix
2 tbsp. mayonnaise
4 tbsp. sweet pickle relish
1 cup finely chopped almonds

Mix cream cheese, chicken, stuffing mix, mayonnaise, and pickle relish. Shape into small balls. Roll balls in crushed almonds. Makes about 3 dozen.

RYE ROUNDS

1 lb. pork sausage
1 lb. ground beef
1 tsp. oregano
1 tsp. basil
¼ tsp. onion powder
¼ tsp. garlic powder
1 lb. Velveeta cheese
40 small rye rounds

Brown sausage and ground beef. Stir to break up as it browns. Drain. Add oregano, basil, onion powder, garlic powder, and chopped cheese. Stir till cheese melts. Spread on small rye rounds. Put on cookie sheet. Put in 350-degree oven for about 10 minutes, till well heated.

MEAT BALLS WITH SPICY CHILI SAUCE

1 lb. ground chuck
1 egg, lightly beaten
1 tbsp. soy sauce
¼ tsp. black pepper
¼ cup dry bread crumbs
¼ cup chopped green onion
½ tsp. salt

In mixing bowl, stir together all meat ball ingredients. Shape into 1-inch balls. Place meat balls in baking pan. Bake in 450-degree oven 10 to 15 minutes, until brown. Makes 5 dozen meat balls.

SPICY CHILI SAUCE

¾ cup bottled chili sauce
1 tbsp. dried onion flakes
2 tbsp. lemon juice
½ tsp. hot pepper sauce
¼ tsp. dry mustard
2 tsp. vinegar
2 tbsp. salad oil
1 tsp. brown sugar
¼ tsp. salt

Mix all sauce ingredients together in saucepan. Bring to a boil and simmer about 5 minutes. Pour over meat balls. Serve as hors d'oeuvres with forks or toothpicks.

SAUSAGE BALLS

1 lb. hot pork sausage
3 cups biscuit baking mix
1 cup shredded cheddar cheese
2 eggs, beaten

Combine all ingredients. Shape into small balls. Place in lightly greased baking pan. Bake in 350-degree oven for 20 minutes, or until light brown. Makes 3 dozen.

POPCORN BALLS

2 cups sugar
¾ cup light corn syrup
¾ cup water
1 tsp. salt
½ cup margarine
1 tsp. vanilla
3 qt. popped corn

Combine sugar, corn syrup, water, and salt in a heavy saucepan. Place over medium heat, stirring till sugar is dissolved. Cook, without stirring, until syrup forms a hard ball when dropped in cold water, or till candy thermometer registers 250 degrees. Remove from heat, then add margarine and vanilla. Put popped corn in large pan. Pour hot syrup over top, mixing well. Grease hands with margarine. Shape into balls. Place on greased cookie sheet to dry and harden. Makes 10 2½-inch balls.

1930s AFTER-SCHOOL SNACKS

BUTTER, SUGAR, AND BREAD

These were our after-school snacks, as we didn't have chips, dips, candy bars, or pizza to snack on. We ate the snacks we did have cold; however, since we are now blessed with the convenience of the electric oven and microwave, you may want to heat them.

Cold biscuits
Butter, softened
Sugar

Split biscuits in half. Spread with butter. Sprinkle sugar over butter. Eat cold, or heat in 350-degree oven or microwave until hot and butter is melted.

MILK AND CORN BREAD

Cold corn bread
Milk

Crumble corn bread in large glass or mug. Pour milk over. Eat with a spoon. Delicious.

HOLE-IN-A-BISCUIT SNACK

Mama never made yeast breads, I suppose because it was too time-consuming. Therefore, a leftover biscuit was our only bread for snacks. Hole-in-a-Biscuit was an easy after-school snack; however, we were in trouble if we let molasses drop out on Mama's kitchen floor.

1 biscuit
Molasses
1 clean finger

With clean finger, make a hole in the side of biscuit. Work finger around to gouge out some of the center. Pour molasses into hole. Better go outside to eat!

PICKLED EGGS

12 hard-boiled eggs
2 cups white vinegar
2 tbsp. sugar
1 tsp. salt
1 tsp. pickling spice
1 onion, peeled and sliced

To cook eggs, put in large pan. Cover with water. Bring to a boil. Put on tight-fitting lid. Remove from heat and let set 15 minutes. Peel eggs and place in quart jars. Combine remaining ingredients in an enamel pan. Heat to boiling. Reduce heat. Simmer 5 minutes. Pour over eggs. Put lids on jars and refrigerate. Good for snacks, garnishes, or salads.

STUFFED EGGS

12 hard-boiled eggs
¼ tsp. salt
¼ tsp. black pepper
3 tbsp. mayonnaise
1 tsp. prepared mustard
1 tbsp. sweet pickle relish
1 tsp. paprika

Peel eggs. Cut in half lengthwise. Put yolks in bowl. Mash and mix with remaining ingredients, except paprika. Fill egg whites with yolk mixture. Sprinkle with paprika.

TUNA SANDWICH SPREAD

Our son was preparing to enter college and he asked me to teach him to cook. Since tuna salad was one of his favorite sandwich spreads, I thought it a simple first lesson. He said, "Okay, what do I do first?" I placed two eggs in a saucepan and said, "Cover these with water and put them on to boil." He gave me a quizzical look and said, "Shouldn't I peel them first?"

As I burst into laughter, he said, "What did I say? What did I say? Why are you laughing?"

"Tim, how could you possibly peel the eggs before they are boiled?"

"Wait a minute, Mother. I'm sure I've seen you boiling eggs and they didn't have the shell on them." Suddenly it dawned on me he had seen me making poached eggs. Still, I could see teaching Tim to cook was going to be more difficult than I imagined.

1 can tuna, drained
2 hard-boiled eggs
½ cup chopped celery
¼ cup chopped dill pickle or sweet
   pickle
3 tbsp. mayonnaise

Mix all together. Spread between 2 slices of bread. Serve with potato chips. For egg salad sandwiches, omit tuna. For chicken salad sandwiches, substitute chopped chicken for tuna.

MINIATURE CREAM PUFFS

1 cup boiling water
½ cup butter
1 cup all-purpose flour
4 eggs

Pour water into small saucepan. Add butter and bring to a boil. Add flour all at once, stirring until mixture leaves sides of pan. Remove from heat. Add eggs one at a time. Eggs will be difficult to beat in. Beat thoroughly after each addition. Drop by teaspoonfuls onto ungreased baking sheet about 1 inch apart. Bake in 425-degree oven 30 minutes, or until brown. Remove to wire racks to cool.

DEVILED CHEESE FILLING

1 cup shredded American cheese
¼ tsp. dry mustard
3 tbsp. mayonnaise
½ tsp. Worcestershire sauce
1 tsp. grated onion
6 drops Tabasco sauce
1 3-oz. can deviled ham

Mix all filling ingredients together. Split cream puffs and fill. Makes 3 dozen.

Breads and Beverages

Me at ten years old, with my nephew Johnnie Stokes and brother Don Lock.

BEST ROLLS

2 pkg. dry yeast
½ cup warm water (105 to 115
**   degrees)**
1½ cups milk
½ cup sugar
2 tsp. salt
¼ cup butter or margarine
5½ cups plain flour
1 egg, beaten
Melted butter

Dissolve yeast in warm water. Set aside. Scald milk. Add sugar, salt, and butter, stirring until butter melts. Cool to lukewarm. Add 2 cups flour. Beat till smooth. Add yeast mixture and beaten egg. Beat well. Stir in remaining flour. Turn out on lightly floured board. Knead until smooth.

Put in well-greased bowl, turning to grease all sides. Cover with clean dish towel. Let rise until doubled, which will take about 1½ hours. Punch down. Knead again. Roll out and cut with biscuit cutter. Put in buttered pan. Brush tops with melted butter. Cover. Let rise again till doubled. Bake in 400-degree oven for 10 to 12 minutes, until brown. Makes about 2½ dozen rolls.

CRACKLIN CORN MUFFINS

Cracklins can be bought in some Southern grocery stores. They are not as good as those we had after rendering out our lard, but they will do. If you can't find cracklins, you can make your own from pork fat chopped into small pieces and fried crisp.

2 cups self-rising cornmeal
1 tsp. sugar
¼ tsp. baking soda
3 eggs
1 cup buttermilk
2 tbsp. butter or margarine,
melted
1 cup cracklins
Flour

Mix together cornmeal, sugar, and baking soda. Set aside. Beat eggs. Add buttermilk and butter. Stir into cornmeal mixture. Stir in cracklins. Spray muffin pans with cooking spray. Dust with flour. Fill ¾ full. Bake in 400-degree oven for 15 to 18 minutes, until brown. Makes 16 muffins.

CORN FRITTERS

3 eggs, separated
1½ cups canned whole-kernel
corn, drained
½ tsp. salt
⅛ tsp. pepper
¼ cup all-purpose flour
6 tbsp. cooking oil

Beat egg yolks. Add corn, salt, pepper, and flour. Beat egg whites until stiff peaks form. Fold into corn mixture. Drop by tablespoon into hot oil in skillet. Brown on both sides, about 2 to 3 minutes on each side. Makes about 3 dozen.

CORN BREAD

2 cups self-rising cornmeal
¼ tsp. baking soda
2 tsp. sugar
1½ cups buttermilk
1 egg, beaten
1 tbsp. margarine, melted
2 tbsp. oil or shortening
Flour

Mix together cornmeal, baking soda, and sugar. Add buttermilk, beaten egg, and margarine. Heat oil in iron skillet. Remove from heat. Sprinkle bottom of skillet with flour. This will keep the bread from sticking. Pour in bread mixture. Bake in 425-degree oven for 25 minutes, or till brown.

Variations: For muffins or corn sticks, pour batter into well-greased and flour-dusted muffin pans or corn stick pans. Bake 15 to 20 minutes until brown.

For fried corn bread, pour 2 or 3 tablespoons batter onto hot greased griddle or skillet. Fry until brown on one side. Turn to brown on other side.

For Mexican corn bread, stir into batter 1 cup shredded cheddar cheese, 1 cup drained whole-kernel corn, and ½ cup green chilies. Bake in skillet as directed above.

SHORTENIN' BREAD

2 cups all-purpose flour
½ tsp. cinnamon
¼ tsp. nutmeg
½ tsp. baking soda
½ cup buttermilk
⅓ cup butter
1 cup molasses
1 egg, beaten

Combine flour, cinnamon, and nutmeg. Dissolve baking soda in buttermilk. Place butter and molasses in heavy saucepan. Bring to a boil, stirring constantly. Add to flour mixture. Stir in buttermilk and egg. Pour batter into a greased and floured 10-inch iron skillet. Bake in 350-degree oven for 25 to 30 minutes, or until wooden pick inserted in center comes out clean. Cool in skillet 10 minutes. Turn out on serving plate. Good when served hot with fresh churned butter. Serves 8.

HUSH'N-UP PUPPIES

1½ cups self-rising cornmeal
1 tsp. sugar
¼ tsp. baking soda
½ cup chopped onion
1 egg
¾ cup buttermilk
Oil

Mix cornmeal, sugar, and baking soda. Add onion. Beat egg and add buttermilk. Stir into cornmeal mixture. Drop by teaspoonfuls into hot oil. Fry till brown on each side. Watch closely—it only takes about 3 minutes to brown on each side. Makes 3 dozen.

GRITS SPOON BREAD

2 cups milk
⅓ cup quick grits
½ tsp. salt
3 eggs, separated
⅓ cup melted butter or margarine

In heavy saucepan over medium heat, scald milk. Combine grits and salt. Stir into milk. Cook, stirring constantly until very thick. Let cool. Stir in beaten egg yolks. Beat egg whites until stiff. Fold into grits. Put butter in a 1½-quart casserole. Spoon in grits. Bake in 350-degree oven for 40 to 45 minutes, until light brown. Serve hot with gravy. Serves 6.

SOUTHERN SPOON BREAD

2½ cups milk
1 cup self-rising cornmeal
2 tbsp. butter or margarine
4 eggs, separated
1 tsp. sugar

Scald milk. Slowly stir in cornmeal. Continue to cook and stir until mixture is thick. Remove from heat. Stir in butter. Beat egg yolks. Add sugar. Stir into cornmeal mixture. Beat egg whites until stiff. Fold into mixture. Bake in greased 2-quart deep baking dish in 375-degree oven for 45 minutes. Serves 6.

HAND-SQUASHED BISCUITS

Ray was an old school chum of Willie's who moved to Chicago and married a Yankee girl. She only made biscuits of the canned variety, so when he came to Tennessee for a visit he really enjoyed my hand-squashed biscuits. He would invariably ask, "Did you wash your hands before you made these?" I would reply, "No, the dough is a great hand-cleaner." Ray either presumed I was kidding, or he liked the biscuits so well he didn't care.

4 cups self-rising flour
⅛ tsp. baking soda
1 cup buttermilk
⅓ cup shortening

Put the flour in deep bowl. Make a well in center of flour. Mix baking soda with buttermilk. Pour in flour well. Drop in shortening. You will not use all the flour. Squeeze and work with hand until shortening is worked in and there is enough flour to have soft dough, but some you can handle.

Turn out on floured board. Knead until smooth. Pat out to about ½ inch. Cut with biscuit cutter or whatever you have available. I use a can with a hole in the top for air. Put 2 tablespoons melted shortening in bread pan. When putting biscuits in, turn to grease both top and bottom. Bake at 450 degrees for about 20 minutes, or until brown. Makes about 12 biscuits.

PONE BREAD

1 tbsp. sugar
½ tsp. baking soda
3 cups self-rising cornmeal
2½ cups boiling water
1 cup buttermilk
1 cup self-rising flour
1¼ cups molasses

Add sugar and baking soda to cornmeal. Pour boiling water over cornmeal, mixing with electric mixer until well blended. Add buttermilk, flour, and molasses, beating well. Pour into a greased and floured tube pan. Bake in 250-degree oven for 3 hours. Cool slightly before removing from pan. Serves 10.

APPLE JULEP

1 qt. unsweetened apple juice
2 cups unsweetened pineapple
   juice
2 cups unsweetened orange juice
½ cup lemon juice
2 tsp. sugar substitute

Combine all ingredients, mixing well. Serve over ice in ½-cup punch cups. Serves 16.

COWBOY COFFEE

There was no metal basket in Mama's large blue-speckled coffee-pot. It was not a percolator. Mama made coffee each morning by filling the pot with water, dumping in the coffee, then putting it on the stove to boil. The pot stayed on the back of the stove all day, the coffee getting stronger and stronger as the day wore on.

Papa drank coffee nearly every meal. He always drank from a saucer, whether the coffee was hot, lukewarm, or cold. In the summer the cookstove was not kept burning all day, so his coffee would be cold for supper. He poured it from the cup into the saucer anyway. I loved to watch Papa drink his coffee. He would tilt the saucer just right so as not to spill a drop.

Not long before he died, Papa was hospitalized. When Top came to visit him one morning, he said, "Papa, is there anything I can do for ya?" His breakfast tray was there with a mug of coffee on it. Papa said, "Yeah, you can get me some cowboy coffee. I can't drink this watered-down stuff." Top insisted he try the coffee on his tray even though he had to drink it from a mug. Soon after I gave Mama an electric coffeepot. Papa drank the coffee and didn't complain, but ever' so often he would dig out the old pot and make cowboy coffee. Here's how to do it.

4 cups water
5 tbsp. coarse ground coffee

Put water in saucepan or old-fashioned coffeepot. Add coffee. Let come to a boil. Simmer 5 minutes or longer—the longer, the stronger. You'll get a few grounds in the bottom of your cup. I like that. Ever' so often, like Papa used to, I get a hankering for cowboy coffee.

BOILED CUSTARD

Mama made boiled custard every Christmas. Since she had no punch bowl, it was served in the dish pan in which it was prepared and dipped out with a dipper. The egg whites floating on top looked like clouds and each cup served contained some of the egg whites. I loved it, although it made a mustache that I couldn't quite lick off.

6 eggs, separated
1 cup sugar
2 qt. milk
1 tsp. vanilla

Beat egg yolks. Add sugar. Slowly add milk, mixing well. Put in large pot. Cook on medium heat, stirring occasionally, until it comes to a boil. Remove from heat. Fold in stiffly beaten egg whites and vanilla. Let whites float in chunks on top. Serve cold. Dip into cups with ladle so as to have egg whites floating on top of each serving. Serves 8 to 10.

SPRING COOLER

1½ cups sugar
2 cups water
1 can (46 oz.) unsweetened
  pineapple juice
2 cups unsweetened orange juice
1 cup lemon juice
1 bottle (33 oz.) ginger ale

Combine sugar and water in saucepan. Bring to a boil and boil 5 minutes. Remove from heat. Add juices and chill. Just before serving, add ginger ale. Serve over ice or thoroughly chilled in ½-cup punch cups. Serves 30.

OLD-TIMEY LEMONADE

When I was a child lemons were very expensive and not always available, so it was a real treat when we had lemonade. Mama only made it on the Fourth of July. It was made in a five-gallon churn with a big chunk of ice in the bottom and the water dipper to dip it up with.

It must have taken at least three dozen lemons and a considerable amount of sugar to make that much lemonade. This is a basic recipe for old-timey lemonade. It would need to be multiplied many times to make a churnful.

> 1½ cups lemon juice
> 1½ cups sugar
> 4 cups boiling water
> 4 or more cups cold water, to
>   taste
> Lemon rinds

Mix lemon juice, sugar, and boiling water. Stir till sugar dissolves. Pour mixture into gallon jug. Add cold water and throw in some of the lemon rinds. Stir well. Pour over ice in 10- to 12-ounce glasses. Serves 12.

PURPLE COW

> 3 scoops vanilla ice cream
> 1 bottle grape soda

Put ice cream in tall glass. Fill with grape soda. Serve with long-handled spoon and straw.

SASSAFRAS TEA

Scrub sassafras roots. Cut into 2- to 3-inch pieces. Place in deep pan. Cover with water and boil about 10 to 15 minutes. Strain. Add hot water to make desired strength. Add sugar and lemon to taste. Good served hot with fried corn bread, butter, and sorghum molasses.

Memoirs

My first-grade class, 1938. I am in the second row, first from left.

Me wearing a country girl outfit in the backyard of my home.

I'M A COUNTRY GIRL

I've milked cows, slopped hogs, gathered eggs, toted in stove wood, fed chickens and dressed them for Sunday dinner. I've churned butter, picked blackberries and poke sallet, shelled bushels of peas and beans, and peeled tubs of tomatoes and peaches for canning. I'm a country girl.

I've worn feed-sack dresses and flour-sack bloomers. I've drawn water from a well, washed clothes on a rub board, and ironed with a flat iron heated on a wood stove. I've slept on feather beds and heard the crickets sing, frogs croak, whippoorwills call, bobwhites and hoot owls and the rooster crow at dawn, all sounds of the country. I've watched a mother bird feed her young and nudge them out of the nest when they were ready to fly. I'm a country girl.

I've pulled one end of a crosscut saw, driven a team of mules, and pulled the down row at corn gathering (the down row is the row of corn that a wagon has driven over). I know the wonderful feeling of a cool breeze while sitting down to rest under the big cottonwood tree at the end of the row. The smell of fresh picked cotton is still in my nostrils. Riding home on a wagonload of cotton after a hard day of picking was like a gentle massage. I remember stealing away to the hayloft on Sunday afternoons, lying in the hay and dreaming of the future. The knowledge gained growing up on a farm with a big family cannot be taught in a classroom. I'm a country girl. Thank God I'm a country girl!

A SPECIAL TIME

Papa went into town once a month to buy supplies. This was a big day for all of us; besides the necessities—flour, sugar, coffee, and cornmeal—he always got a special treat for everyone. For the kids under ten years old, he bought candy. It was usually orange slices, chocolate drops, and stick candy. The older kids got tablets with movie stars' pictures on the front, pencils, and an occasional box of crayons to be shared. He always brought Mama an Orange Crush and a Western romance. Papa would scold Mama terribly if he caught her giving even a sip of her Orange Crush to any of us kids. That was her special treat, something he couldn't afford to buy for all of us.

Mama and Papa worked so hard taking care of the kids and working the farm. We were poor, but always had plenty to eat. We raised red potatoes, sweet potatoes, corn, tomatoes, beans, peas, turnips, watermelon, and cantelopes. Mama canned enough vegetables to do us all winter. Papa killed enough hogs and the boys hunted so that we had plenty of ham and other meat. We had cows to provide us with lots of milk and butter. Our chickens gave us eggs and meat to eat.

We also had nice clothes. Mama had a treadle sewing machine (one that is run without electricity) and could sew like a dream. When she had no money to buy material she would use the printed sacks that cattle feed came in.

We had a lot of company, but if no company was expected and everything was going smoothly, Mama and Papa would take what they called their "day off." It was usually on Saturday or Sunday afternoon, after dinner. Each child was assigned a chore. The dishes were

Mama, 1940.   *Papa, 1938.*

to be washed and put away and the little kids taken care of for the afternoon. Mama and Papa would then go into the parlor, Mama with her Western romance or her crochet, Papa with his pipe and ledger book. The door was never locked, but we were not to go into the parlor unless it was an emergency.

I loved to peep in the screen door or the window. Sometimes Mama would be reading and Papa would be lying on the divan sleeping. Sometimes Papa would be working on his ledger book or they would just be talking. I once saw them sitting close together on the divan holding hands. If they saw us looking through the window or door they would smile and wave, then go on about their business. We were never scolded for peeping by anyone but my older sister, who was in charge. Mama once heard her scolding us terribly for peeping. She told us it was all right, but for us to go play and enjoy our day. This was Mama's and Papa's special time together and a special time for us, too; it made us know that they loved each other and we felt secure in that love.

THE DANCE

Ours was a big two-story house, the porch stretching all the way across the front. The boys slept upstairs. The girls and Mama and Papa slept downstairs.

All the rooms were very large. Papa made a table for the dining room. It was ten feet long and four feet wide with benches on the sides. With two chairs at each end it could seat twelve people or more.

The welcome mat was always out at our house. On Sunday morning Papa would go upstairs and count heads to see how many boys my brothers had invited to spend the night. Mama would then know how much to cook for breakfast. Many times, with the help of my older sisters, Mama would fry a whole ham or a side of middling meat for breakfast, along with three or four dozen eggs and about four dozen biscuits, with sweet milk gravy, red-eye gravy, blackberry jam, and sorghum molasses on the side. Food was no problem. Almost everything we ate was grown or raised, in abundance, on the farm.

Aunt Ibbie, Uncle John, and their 1949 Studebaker.

Summers were busy times working the crops and preparing food for the winter, but when fall rolled around, there was always time left over for fun. One of my earliest recollections was excitement of a dance at our house. Mama and Aunt Ibbie were feverishly cleaning house and baking cookies for the big night. The table in the dining room was covered with Mama's best tablecloth and moved up against the wall to make room for dancing. Two five-gallon churns filled with lemonade and dozens of tea cakes were put on the table. The benches and other chairs were lined up along the wall for sitting.

Early in the afternoon people started to arrive. In the shade of the big oak trees the musicians began to warm up. The band consisted of my brother Austin, who played the guitar and sang; Uncle Sam on fiddle; a cousin who blew a horn; and another cousin on guitar. Requested songs were played, with people sitting on the edge of the porch dangling their feet, clapping and singing along until it began to get dark. Everyone then moved inside and the dancing began.

Mama said us kids could stay up and watch the dancing if we would stay out of the way. She gave my sister, little brother, and me a glass of lemonade and some tea cakes and sat us down under the big table. This gave us a very good view of the dancing feet.

The band began to play a waltz. When Aunt Ibbie and Uncle John, said to be the best dancers in the county, took the floor, everyone else backed off and watched. After the dance was over everyone clapped and clapped, Johnnie, Don, and I clapping the loudest.

I heard Mama say many times that Aunt Ibbie and Uncle John could dance ever' bit as good as Fred Astaire and Ginger Rogers. The only other time I saw them dance was after they had grown old and grey and I was a teenager. The dance was in the school gym. The band was playing a waltz and Aunt Ibbie and Uncle John were persuaded to dance. They were the only couple on the floor, and as they circled the large gym floor I almost busted with pride. To my eyes they were not only the best dancers in the county, but the best in the whole world.

PORCH SITTING

We all looked forward to porch sitting weather; with twelve people living in the same house the winters got awfully long. We started porch sitting as early as March. We usually had to wear sweaters or light jackets through March and most of April, but it was so good to get out from behind closed doors.

The front porch was the gathering place for most of our social activities. In the late afternoon, after supper and after all chores were done, neighbors would walk for miles to sit and visit. The grown-ups would talk, laugh, and tell stories while the children played games like hide-and-seek, kick-the-can, and wave me out of jail. We liked to go to Aunt Ida's and Uncle Eural's. Uncle Eural had a two-wheeled buggy he let us play with. It was such fun, pulling each other in the buggy— it took two to pull the buggy and two could ride. After dark we would catch fireflies, put them in jars, sit in a circle, and tell ghost stories with the fireflies as our only light.

On Friday and Saturday nights the front porch was reserved for the older girls and their boyfriends. Mama and Papa and the little kids took to the back porch on these nights. Sundays were family and company days on the front porch.

My sisters and I sometimes had slumber parties on the porch. We'd bring out the feather beds and some quilts. Sometimes there would be as many as fifteen girls on that porch. I remember one night we were having a slumber party and four boys rode up on their horses. They were boyfriends of some of the girls. They sat on their horses for a while and talked. All lights were out in the house and they thought sure Papa would be asleep, so they slid down off their horses and started up the porch steps. Papa's voice roared out from behind the screen door: "All right boys, that's far enough. Get on your horses and ride out." It scared the boys so bad they didn't have to be told twice.

Deidra, our five-year-old granddaughter, said, "Granny, why didn't you have your slumber party in the house so you could watch television?" Television is a wonderful invention, one I would not want to be without, but I think it has robbed our children of a lot of imagination and the wonderful fun of porch sitting.

PREACHING ALL DAY AND DINNER ON THE GROUNDS

(Papa said he would much prefer to have dinner all day and preaching on the grounds.)

For this once-a-year event, people began arriving at the church about 9:30 A.M. At least two visiting preachers, as well as our regular once-a-month preacher, would be there.

Joyce and her daddy, Brother Ed Bradley, were the first to arrive. They lived across the road from the church. Brother Ed led the singing and took care of the church house and grounds. Joyce played the piano. She played beautifully, even though she had never had a lesson and could not read music. No one in our community could afford to own a piano. Joyce was very fortunate to live near the church so she could practice.

Aunt Ibbie would arrive with a big bouquet of flowers. They were placed in front of the pulpit for all to admire and enjoy. Aunt Ibbie

Mama and Papa porch sitting. *Lady Boy porch sitting.*

Porch sitting.

Preaching all day and dinner on the grounds. Drawing by
Willie Ledford.

loved flowers, and always managed to have a bouquet for every occasion, including Sunday service. If there were no flowers blooming in her yard, she checked the woods and roadsides for Sweet Williams, lady's slippers, daisies, and Queen Anne's lace.

About fifteen minutes before the service was to begin, Joyce would start playing the piano. The beautiful music lured the people into the church house. By 10:00, the hugs and handshakes taken care of, everyone would settle down for singing and preaching. Brother Ed invited anyone who so desired to join the choir and lead in the singing. It was not a formal or rehearsed choir. Aunt Ibbie's strong alto voice blended in so beautifully with the other singers that I felt sure the angels in Heaven could not have sounded sweeter.

The songs, "Count Your Blessings," "Revive Us Again," and "When the Roll Is Called Up Yonder" were almost always sung. Even the little kids were included in the service. Miss Nellie, the first-, second-, and third-grade teacher of the community school, also taught the little ones in Sunday school. The mothers and fathers watched with great pride as the group from age two to about eight marched up front and sang "Jesus Loves Me" and "I'll Be a Sunbeam," with Miss Nellie directing.

Brother Billy would be the first to preach, as the visiting preachers were saved for the afternoon. He would start off reading the Bible and talking real calm and softlike. As he progressed further into the sermon, he'd begin to talk louder and louder, jamming his fist into his outstretched hand. Sometimes he scared me, but I dared not move. If I did, Mama gave me a look that meant I'd better be still and quiet.

After a while, and many "amens," Brother Billy would calm down, his voice getting real low and sweet. He'd tell us how Jesus died on the cross for each and every one of us, and how Jesus could save us from hell if we'd come down the aisle, confess our sins, and ask His forgiveness. The choir sang "Just As I Am" as some people walked down the aisle.

The close of the service was a joyous occasion, with the choir singing "Ring the Bells of Heaven," Brother Ed directing and clapping his hands, and people hugging and crying over those who had been saved. After emotions were exhausted, the womenfolk prepared the dinner outside under the trees, while the menfolk talked about the crops and other business. The ladies brought their best tablecloths to cover the large homemade tables. So much food was prepared we could truly have eaten all day. After everyone had their fill, we'd go back into the church house, and the singing and preaching would begin again.

Preaching all day and dinner on the grounds was the event of the year, a day looked forward to, a day when families and friends were united in fellowship and love. If only there was a way to have every man, woman, and child in America attend an old-fashioned preaching all day and dinner on the grounds once a year. I think we'd have a crime-free nation and a happier people.

SCRIPTURE CAKE

1 cup butter or margarine	: Judg. 5:25
2 cups sugar	: Jer. 6:20
1 tbsp. honey	: Exod. 16:31
6 eggs	: Isa. 10:14
3½ cups flour, divided	: 1 Kings 4:22
2 tsp. baking powder	: 1 Cor. 5:6
½ tsp. salt	: Lev. 2:13
½ tsp. cinnamon	: 1 Kings 10:10
¼ tsp. cloves	: 1 Kings 10:10
⅛ tsp. ginger	: 1 Kings 10:10
1 cup water	: Exod. 17:6
2 cups figs, chopped	: 1 Sam. 30:12
2 cups golden raisins	: 1 Sam. 30:12
1 cup almonds	: Gen. 43:11

Cream together butter, sugar, and honey. Add eggs one at a time, beating well after each addition. Sift together 3 cups of the flour, baking powder, salt, and spices. Add to creamed mixture alternately with water, beginning and ending with flour.

Dredge figs, raisins, and almonds in the remaining ½ cup flour. Stir into batter. Spoon batter into greased and floured 9-by-5-inch loaf pan. Bake in 325-degree oven for 1½ hours, or until wooden pick inserted in center comes out clean. Cool in pan for 10 minutes. Turn out on wire rack to cool.

D DAY: MAY 1ST

From the time the first crocus pushed its way out from under the snow, we began to look forward to the first day of May. May 1st was

D day for us, the day we were allowed to pull off our winter underwear and shoes and go barefoot. No matter how warm the weather was in April, Mama was convinced if we didn't wear our winter underwear until the first day of May we would "ketch" pneumonia and die.

When we first removed that scratchy old underwear, it gave our bodies such a liberated feeling. We always hoped Papa would be plowing so we could feel the fresh-turned earth on our bare feet, or that it would rain and leave puddles to wade in. Someone would invariably cut his or her foot on the first day. Mama would wash it out and pour coal oil on it, then put a piece of salt meat over the sore and wrap it with a flour-sack rag. The salt meat would draw the poison and keep it from swelling. This was the way she treated all infections, and it really worked.

We went barefoot all summer. After a few days our feet would toughen. Our one pair of shoes were saved for Sunday school. If we didn't outgrow them they would be good enough to start school in. Going barefoot was a real money saver, but we preferred going barefoot to wearing shoes anyway.

We would occasionally try to sneak into bed at night without washing our feet, but never got away with it. Mama would check every night to see if our feet were clean before we got into bed. Mama took seriously the saying, "Cleanliness is next to godliness." The beds and the house were to be kept clean. She was really more concerned about keeping the bedclothes clean than whether or not we had clean feet. With so many people in the house, it was necessary to have rules; otherwise the house would have been like a pig sty.

THE MESSAGE

The new Piggly Wiggly store was the talk of the community. Before now all grocery stores had clerks to get the merchandise for you. You'd tell him what you wanted, or give him a list, and he'd pick it from the shelves. The new Piggly Wiggly had carts to push up and down the aisles. You could look to your heart's content and select whatever you wanted from the shelves, put it in your basket, and pay for it when you got to the front of the store.

Mama had a ball in that store. She didn't buy much, for she felt she should stay loyal to Mr. Rucker and buy most of the groceries at his place, but she sure had fun looking. If Papa ran low of cash before the crops came in, he could always charge what we needed at Rucker's Grocery. One thing Mr. Rucker didn't have that Mama bought at Piggly Wiggly was penny drink. It was like Kool-Aid, but only cost a penny for an envelope.

Mama made up a batch of orange penny drink one hot spring day, put some in a jug, and sent Johnnie and me to the field where Papa and Top were plowing. It would be a refreshing treat for them and we didn't mind the walk. We liked to walk barefoot in the fresh-plowed ground.

We met Papa and Top at the end of a row. After enjoying their treat and emptying the jug, Johnnie and I started back to the house. We were about halfway across the field, walking slowly, letting the dirt filter through our toes and arguing over who should carry the empty jug, when I looked up at the clear blue sky and saw what I thought was a bird with smoke coming out of its tail. It was making letters in the sky!

This really frightened us. We knew birds couldn't write without the help of the Lord. We had been so bad lately, fussing and fighting, He was probably having the bird write a message to us for all the world to see. We began to run, but the letters just kept coming, seeming to follow us. When we reached the house we told Mama to come look. The world must be coming to an end, as Brother Billy had warned, and God was having a bird write a message in the sky. By that time the message was completed: "Drink Red Top Beer." When Mama saw it, she began to laugh and said, "Girls, you have nothing to be frightened of. I'm sure God would never write such a message as that." It was only an airplane with smoke coming out the back. We knew about airplanes, but the plane had been flying so high we could barely see it and couldn't hear its motor. We'd never seen the like.

Mama said it could have been a message from God; he could make a bird write in the sky if He wanted to, and we had better behave ourselves and be nicer to each other. This experience had a definite effect on Johnnie and me. We didn't fuss and fight so much for a while.

HALLOWEEN

It was Halloween, and my cousin Nellie was spending the night with me. We wanted to go trick-or-treating, but we had no masks. Money was never wasted on such foolish things as store-bought Halloween masks. Mama said we'd have to make our own.

She gave us each a flour sack, scissors, and crayons. The sacks fit perfectly over our heads. The places needed for eyes and mouth were carefully marked out, cut, and painted. We put our masks on and began to pester Mama to let us go to my brother Chock's house about a quarter of a mile away. We planned to peek in the window and scare them. Mama warned us it was a dark night and we may be afraid. Nellie and I assured her we weren't afraid; after all, we weren't babies anymore. We were ten years old.

As we walked down the road we didn't feel at all afraid. The moon would peek out every so often from behind the clouds to light our way. When we reached Chock's house we peeked in the window, showed our masked faces, then ducked down, trying to muffle our giggles.

Chock must have suspected the goblins to be Nellie and me, for as we were getting ready to peer into the window again he slipped up behind us, grabbed us, and yelled, "Boo!" It scared the living daylights out of us. Chock picked us up, one under each arm, and carried us into the house, where Mae had tea cakes and milk waiting.

After our fill and Chock's offer to walk us home, which we declined, we started back. We were giggling and talking when we heard a rustling in the bushes. Suddenly two white-clad figures lunged up out of the bushes by the roadside. They looked like what I had been told ghosts looked like. We turned and began to run. My body tried to outrun my legs. I stumbled and fell. Being so frightened, I must have blacked out for a moment. When I opened my eyes, the ghosts had me cradled in their arms, only they looked a lot like my sisters Margaret and Brownie with sheets draped over them. They had meant to scare us, but never dreamed it would be so traumatic for us. They made a pack saddle and carried me home with Nellie holding on to their skirts. The pack saddle ride home was almost worth the scare.

AUNT LIZZIE'S CURE

One day while playing outside, I must have disturbed a bumblebees' nest, for one of them stung me on the neck. Lucky for me, Aunt Lizzie, the only snuff-dipper in the family, was visiting us. She stuck her finger under her lip, dug out a gob of wet snuff, and dabbed it on my neck. I said, "Ugh," and tried to pull away, but Aunt Lizzie held on to me with one hand and held the snuff in place with the other. She said, "Be still child. This will take the sting out." And so it did. There was never any swelling, and I hardly knew I had ever been stung, but the cure was almost worse than the bite.

Aunt Lizzie's snuff glasses were our drinking glasses. She kept us well supplied. I have a snuff glass, complete with lid, in the top of my cabinet. I wish it was one of Aunt Lizzie's glasses, but none of them

Aunt Lizzie.

survived. I bought my treasured glass at a yard sale for twenty-five cents. I would gladly have paid much more. It was exactly like Aunt Lizzie's, and the first of its kind I had seen in a long time. I would happily trade my beautiful eight-piece crystal glass set for a set of Aunt Lizzie's snuff glasses.

SWEET LITTLE TOM

Mama always said Little Tom was the best baby she had; he seldom cried. Having no cradle or baby bed, Mama put pillows around Little Tom, and with the bed pushed against the wall she felt sure he would be safe while sleeping even though he was at the age of scooting around and rolling over.

One day Mama had a lot of work to do, and thought while the baby was sleeping would be a good time to go to the garden and pick beans for dinner. She picked hurriedly and was only out in the garden for ten or fifteen minutes. The baby usually slept at least an hour, but not this time.

When she returned to the house to check on Little Tom he had somehow managed to crawl over the pillows and slip down between the bed and the wall. Mama longed to hear him crying for once, but he couldn't. Mama was frantic. She began trying to breathe life into him, and she ran with him in her arms to the field where Papa was plowing. They could never revive him. His little neck was broken.

Mama was devastated. She always blamed herself. She tortured herself the rest of her life by saying, "I had ten children, but I let one of them get killed."

DESIGNER ORIGINALS

Mama could have been a famous dress designer. She never used pencil and sketch pad, but cut her patterns with scissors and newspaper. These designs were often all her own, but sometimes taken from

*At the country store. I am in the front row in my green
dress with pink smocking.*

pictures in the Sears and Roebuck Catalogue, or from dresses on the
rack at Salenfriend's or Graber's department stores.

It was amazing what Mama could do with a piece of fabric. With
talented fingers and her old treadle sewing machine, I truly believe she
could have made a silk purse out of a sow's ear. Aunt Ibbie often
added touches of embroidery and smocking to our clothes. The pale
green dress with a pink smocked yolk, and the blue and white print
pinafore with hat and drawstring bag to match made from feed sacks
are stamped forever in my memory. Mama never put labels on her
designer originals. She never made any money from her expertise.
Her reward for her work could be seen in her eyes when her daughters
proudly wore the latest fashions.

Another original I shall always remember was designed by Chock,
the clown of the family. It was a bathing suit with a Purina label. Water
was scarce so we often took shower baths when a summer shower
erupted. Having no bathing suits, we played in the rain with our
clothes on and, using a bar of P. and G. soap, washed clothes and
bodies at the same time.

One day, in anticipation of a rainstorm, Chock decided to make
himself a bathing suit. Using a tow sack—burlap bags cattle feed came
in—he cut a hole in the top for his head and a hole in each side for

his arms. Another sack was cut in two places for his legs, pulled up, and tied around the waist with a rope. Just as the rain began Chock came prancing down the back steps. Of course he got a big laugh out of us kids.

Every time I see a fashion show I think of Mama bent over her sewing machine, sometimes working far into the night to finish a dress I thought I had to wear the next day, and of Chock coming down the back steps in his designer original with a Purina label.

THE SANITARY TOILET

Many families were so poor in the thirties and early forties that they

The sanitary toilet. Drawing by Willie Ledford.

didn't even have an outhouse, our family being one of them. Most of us had our own special hiding place in or behind the barn.

One day Margaret was helping Johnnie with her first-grade reading lesson. The story was about farm animals. Johnnie read, "The cow was in the...," and as she came to the word "barn," she hesitated. Instead of telling Johnnie the word, intending to give her a hint, Margaret said, "Where do you go when you have to be excused?" Johnnie read the sentence again: "The...cow...was...in...the...tater...patch." Johnnie and Margaret had definitely not been going to the same place.

Soon after Franklin Roosevelt was elected president, the unsanitary situation of the rural people came to his attention. He declared that every rural residence should have an outhouse. Until this time all outhouses had been shacks with dirt floors. The "sanitary toilet" had a concrete floor and was painted redwood.

We were so proud of our sanitary toilet. The chore of keeping the outhouse swept out and clean was assigned each week. Since no toilet paper was available to us, we used an old Sears and Roebuck Catalogue.

THE LIGHTS

It was 1938, a very exciting time for our community. Plumbing and electricity had not yet entered our lives in rural west Tennessee. President Roosevelt had passed the Rural Electrification Act and we were getting the lights. We could not foresee the future of electric appliances and other electrical devices. The wonderful bright lights were our only knowledge of electricity.

Word was passed along each day as to how far the workmen had gotten. "The Davises got the lights yesterday; maybe they would get to our house today." The dreaded chore of cleaning chimneys and filling the oil lamps would be a thing of the past. We'd not need those old-fashioned lamps anymore.

Our first electric appliance was an iron. Those old-fashioned flat irons that had to be heated on the stove could be thrown away or used for doorstops.

When Papa carried the first bale of cotton to the gin that fall, he would buy an electric radio. Where could we hide the old battery-operated Truetone? It looked more like a cathedral than a radio. We wouldn't want anyone to think we were still using that old-fashioned thing.

THE REFRIGERATOR

Cousin Dixie was bragging to everyone at school about the electric refrigerator her daddy had just bought. She was having a birthday party and her mother was going to serve ice cream made in the new refrigerator. I could not understand how this was possible. The only way Mama could make ice cream was by using our old hand-cranked ice-cream freezer with the wooden bucket. How could Dixie's mother get an ice-cream bucket in the refrigerator and crank it at the same time? I was very anxious to go to the party and find out.

I was not interested in the games being played, for my mind was too preoccupied with the ice cream. After the games were finally over, and we sang happy birthday, and Dixie blew out the candles, it was time for the mystery of the ice cream. As Cousin Bertha opened the refrigerator, I was looking closely for the bucket, but instead she took out four shallow, narrow pans of ice cream. They sure didn't hold very much, but it was really good. Maybe not as creamy as Mama's, but this was magical ice cream, made without cranking.

While excitedly telling Papa about the wonders of the refrigerator and the delicious ice cream, I said, "Papa, can't we get a refrigerator?" He said, "We don't need one of them newfangled things. We have a perfectly good icebox, and the iceman runs twice a week."

A NEW WAY TO GOSSIP

There were many firsts for us in the thirties and forties. Our first telephone was an eight-party line. This meant we had to share the line with seven other people. When someone else on the line was using their telephone, we could hear their conversation on our phone.

This was a great gossiping device, but Papa wouldn't allow us to listen in on anyone else's conversations. If we picked up our phone and someone was on the line, we were to hang up immediately. Papa limited all calls to a minute or two. He said the phone was to be used for important calls and farm business only, not for gossiping. That kinda took the fun out of it.

THE CAR

A truck was our only transportation. It was necessary for all farmers to own trucks for hauling, but a truck wasn't the best way of getting the family to town. Only three could sit up front: Mama, Papa, and the youngest. The rest had to ride in the back.

Our beautifully combed hair and pressed clothes would be a mess by the time we got to town. We were embarrassed, especially the girls, so Papa would stop at the Greyhound bus station on the edge of town and we would straighten up in the rest room. When everybody was presentable, we would walk the two blocks into town.

The car.

Finally, Mama and Papa began discussing the possibility of buying a car. Mama pointed out the fact that the girls were getting older and needed a mode of transportation that wouldn't blow their skirts up. Papa said, "We can't afford a new car, but I'll look around."

One day Papa and Austin, the oldest, went into town to look at cars. When they came back Austin was driving the truck and Papa the most beautiful car I had ever seen. It was a dark-green 1937 Ford four-door—not a new car, but all that mattered was we had a car. When we all piled in to go for a ride, it was real crowded, but nobody seemed to mind.

I never wanted to be seen riding in the back of the truck. I always hoped Papa would drive right up town and park on the square where we could be seen in our beautiful car. Oh, how I loved that car!

VACCINATION DAY

Papa and the boys were vaccinating hogs when Top caught Papa all bent over. Not thinking what the consequences could be, he couldn't resist sticking him with the needle right in the hind end. Papa squealed louder than any of the pigs. Top took off running with Papa close behind. When Papa caught up with him he gave Top a good talking to. "I know you wuz just havin' fun, and I don't thank I got enough of the medicine to do any harm, but vaccinatin' is serious business and somethin' like this had better not happen again."

After saying grace at supper Papa pretended to hiccup and let out an oink. The boys fell over with laughter. Papa looked over the table and said, "Eva, don't you have no corn on the table?" The boys again went into a fit of laughter. Chock said, "Maybe there's some slop in the slop bucket, Papa." Mama said, "What is going on here, George?" "Nothin', Eva," Papa said with a wink. "Just a little joke between me and the boys."

That night Papa told Mama about the needle incident. She said, "George, I do declare, you beat all. That boy shoulda had a whuppin' and you jest joke about it." Papa said, "Don't worry, Eva. It won't happen again. Top knows it weren't a very smart thang to do." I heard

Mama tell this story many times. She said she told Papa, "George, if you go to gruntin' and snortin' in your sleep I'm gonna go sleep with one of the youngins."

SATURDAY TREAT

The kids were growing up; there were no more babies in the family. Papa began to take the whole family to town every Saturday. We worked hard all week in the fields and doing chores, so this was a real treat for us.

Sometimes Papa would give each of us a dime. This would buy a double-decker ice-cream cone from the ice-cream parlor. One Saturday, after each of us had bought an ice-cream cone, Mama herded us across the street to the courthouse yard. We all sat down under the trees to eat our ice cream, Mama cautioning us all the time to hold our cones out so we wouldn't get any ice cream on our clothes.

My brother had licked his ice cream down to the cone and was holding it out after each lick when all of a sudden a bird flew over and, plop...right in Don's ice-cream cone. He began to cry and wanted to eat it anyway. Mama carefully tore the top off and saved some of it. Don knew there would be no more ice cream until the next Saturday, and possibly not then. It depended on whether or not Papa could spare a dime for each of us.

WARM SUMMER RAIN

It was a beautiful summer night. The stars and moon were shining. Margaret and her boyfriend, Theo, were sitting on the edge of the porch courting when suddenly what felt like a warm rain came running off the tin roof and splattering on their feet and legs. As they jumped up and ran out into the yard, some splattered onto their heads. Margaret looked up and saw it was coming from the upstairs bedroom where Don slept. She left Theo wiping his head with his handkerchief and stormed into the house.

"What's the matter? Where you goin'?" Mama said. Margaret shouted, "I'm going upstairs to kill Don! He just peed on Theo and me!" Mama said, "How could he do that? He's in bed asleep."

"Out the window, Mama. He did it out the window and it ran down the roof on us. I've never been so embarrassed in my life. I'm going to kill him."

"Now wait a minute, Margaret. I'll take care of Don. You go see what you can do for your guest."

When Mama went into the bedroom, Don had gotten back into bed, not knowing he had done anything wrong. He had probably done this many times before rather than go downstairs and outside.

Margaret washed up, composed herself, and went back out with a towel for Theo, but he had left. Margaret cried and cried and still wanted to kill Don. She thought she would never see Theo again, but he must have been very much in love, for come Saturday night he was back. However, from then on he insisted they do their courting sitting in the porch swing. He even married Margaret. I'd say it takes a lot of courage to marry into a family where one of the members has peed on you.

MAMA AND PAPA GAVE MUCH FOR THEIR COUNTRY: A SON

It was a Saturday night in 1944, time for the Hit Parade, but the president was making a speech about the war, saying how it would soon be over. I was anxious for the war to be over and for Wallace to come home. Mama and Papa worried about him so much, and wanted to hear any news they could, but why couldn't the president speak on another night? I just had to know the number one song of the week. Would it be "Don't Fence Me In," Sentimental Journey," or "Chattanooga Choo Choo"?

I wouldn't find out that night because I didn't dare turn the dial on the radio, and after the speech was over it would be too late to listen

Pfc. George Wallace Lock.

Mama and Papa gave much for their country: a son.

Lewis (my cousin), Wallace, Chock (my brothers), and L. C. Lock (Lewis' brother) and hounds.

to the Hit Parade. I could only hope the station carrying the Hit Parade also had the president's speech on it; then I wouldn't be the only one in school Monday morning who didn't know the number one song. I could hear Mama and Papa talking into the night. I heard Papa say, "Don't worry, Eva, Wallace will be home soon. The war is almost over."

That night I woke up with a start. Someone was screaming, a sound I had never heard before in the middle of the night. I ran into Mama and Papa's room. It was Mama crying and saying, "It was Wallace. I saw him, I saw him." Papa was holding her, rocking back and forth trying to comfort her. Mama kept saying she saw Wallace coming down the road. She was running to meet him and when she got to him he was all covered with blood. "It's a warning, George, I just know it's a warning." Papa kept saying, "It was only a dream, Mama. He'll be home soon, it was only a dream."

One week later our neighbors Cousin Allie and Jim Davis drove up to the house, and a car with "U.S. Marine Corps" written on the side drove in behind them. A man in a uniform got out of the car and introduced himself as chaplain of the naval base in Millington. Mama said, "Allie, it's Wallace, isn't it? I knew it was coming. I had a warning." The chaplain read the telegram out loud, expressed his sympathy, and left. Cousin Allie stayed on and Jim got in his car to go tell other family and friends.

It was a devastating time. Wallace was only nineteen. We never got to see him in his uniform except in pictures. He didn't get to come home after boot camp as was customary. Papa sent money to him at the marine training center in San Diego for train fare, but a telegram arrived on the day he was to leave to come home saying the war was escalating and all leaves had been canceled. He was shipped out that day. He was killed when a grenade hit his foxhole on a tiny island in the Pacific called Peleliu.

I didn't realize the anguish Mama must have suffered until after her death. While going through her papers we found the telegram, ration book, and letters which are printed here. For me, the most heartrending part of the package was the letter sent seven months after his death about the fifty-six cents found on the body. Couldn't they realize it would have been much kinder to have kept the fifty-six cents? I see on the news every day how the U.S. government wastes and mismanages millions of the taxpayers' dollars, but they had to send Mama and Papa that fifty-six cents. Oh, the anguish Mama and Papa must have felt!

After Wallace was killed, Chock, Top, and Austin were very angry. Thus far they had been deferred from the military because they were farmers and had wives and small children. They went to the local enlistment station to volunteer. They felt this would be a way of fighting back for Wallace, but they were all turned down and labeled 4F. Chock had a back problem he didn't know about, Top's eyes didn't pass the test, and Austin had always been sickly.

However, this didn't discourage them. Chock and Austin headed for Detroit to work in defense plants, and Top remained behind to help Papa with the farm. They couldn't fight in the front lines, but did the best they could behind the lines to help defeat the enemy that had taken Wallace's life.

WESTERN
UNION

WASHINGTON DC

MR & MRS GEORGE W LOCK—   1944 OCT 4   PM 9 26

DEEPLY REGRET TO INFORM YOU THAT YOUR SON PRIVATE FIRST CLASS GEORGE W LOCK USMCR WAS KILLED IN ACTION IN THE PERFORMANCE OF HIS DUTY AND SERVICE OF HIS COUNTRY. NO INFORMATION AVAILABLE AT PRESENT REGARDING DISPOSITION OF REMAINS. TEMPORARY BURIAL IN LOCALITY WHERE DEATH OCCURRED PROBABLE. YOU WILL BE PROMPTLY FURNISHED ANY ADDITIONAL INFORMATION RECEIVED TO PREVENT POSSIBLE AID TO OUR ENEMIES DO NOT DIVULGE THE NAME OF HIS SHIP OR STATION. PLEASE ACCEPT MY HEARTFELT SYMPATHY. LETTER FOLLOWS—

A A VANDERGRIFT LIEUT GENERAL USMC COMMANDANT OF THE MARINE CORPS.

HEADQUARTERS U. S. MARINE CORPS

7 May, 1945.

My dear Mrs. Lock:

Enclosed please find fifty-six cents ($0.56) which was found among the personal effects of your son, the late Private First Class George W. Lock, U. S. Marine Corps Reserve, and forwarded to this office for transmittal to you.

Please sign the enclosed receipt and return it to this office in the attached envelope which requires no postage.

Should any other effects be located and identified as the property of your son, they will be forwarded to you as soon as practicable after their receipt.

Sincerely yours,

M. G. CRAIG,
First Lieutenant, U. S. Marine Corps.

MOVING ON UP

Chock and Austin were making much more money than they ever could on the farm, so they stayed on after the war, and Top and his family went north to join them. Papa's health was failing. Only Johnnie, Don, and I remained at home to help with the farm. Papa and Mama struggled with the decision, but finally decided to sell the farm and move to town.

The farm was put up for sale and we began to look for a place in town. I was very excited at the prospect of being a town kid. People who lived in the city were considered of much higher social standards than those of us who lived in the country and worked in the fields. In those days we avoided the sun by wearing wide-brimmed straw hats, scarves around our necks, long sleeves, and gloves. To be tanned and have calloused hands branded you a country hick. I longed to be snake-belly white like a town kid. Boy howdy, have things changed! Young people today pay a lot of money to get a tan, not to avoid one.

The farm soon sold and Papa bought a house in town. It had a bathroom, and a closet in every bedroom. I'd be glad to see the last of the outhouse. Since there was plenty of closet space we'd not need the big hand-carved wardrobe that was Grandma Lock's. It was left in the farmhouse. We got an electric refrigerator, so the beautiful old wooden icebox was also left behind. We wouldn't have a cow in town, so we'd have no use for the two churns and the two wooden buttermolds, one round with a flower mold on it, and one square with a pineapple design. Mama would no longer have any use for the big wash kettle, for there was an electric wringer-washer in her future. We certainly wouldn't need all those old blue fruit jars or the oblong copper canner. The ice tongs, cotton scales, milking stool, corn grinder, flat irons, and oil lamps were all left on the farm. Papa figured the people who bought the farm could use them. We left the well pulley and bucket and the horse collars and harnesses hanging in the barn. I don't know what happened to the battery-operated cathedral radio, the Victrola and Jimmie Rodgers records, or the beautiful old buffet and the table and benches Papa made. I guess they were also left behind. Our new house would have a beautiful red and grey chrome table and chairs in the kitchen, and many built-in cabinets. Our town house must be all modern decor.

What would now be great treasures were at that time old-fashioned things we no longer needed. The Locks were moving on up.

AUTO-ATTRACTION

Being a city kid was not as much fun as I had anticipated. I missed my cousins and other friends. Pat was now my best girl friend. She introduced me to her uncle, my future husband, Willie. He being so much older I never thought he would be interested in me, but at school one day Pat said Willie wanted a date. He was twenty-five years old, had just gotten out of the Navy, and had his own car. I was only sixteen, and I just knew Mama and Papa would never give their permission. Pat said, "We'll ask them." They finally consented, but only if Pat would go with us.

I liked Willie very much. He was more mature than any other boys I had been around, and he had a new 1948 Ford car. I had never ridden in a new car before, and was impressed, to say the least. I told my brothers to be extra nice to him and he might let them ride in his new car. When I asked Top how he liked Willie, he said he liked him okay, but he looked like Jimmy Durante. Willie does have a big nose and Top liked to kid. Papa said, "Who's Jimmy Durante?" When Top explained he was a song-and-dance man in the movies, Papa said, "Now don't be telling her he looks like a movie star or she'll really fall for him."

Willie and I went together almost a year when we began to talk about marriage. Johnnie worked at the telephone company and had gotten a job there for me after school and on Saturdays and Sundays; there was not much time for seeing Willie. I was in love, had a good job, and thought school was a waste of time. I wanted to quit school, get married, and go to work full-time. Papa had his suspicions that a lot of what attracted me to Willie was his new car, and he wanted me to finish school. He promised to buy a new car and let me drive it if I would just wait until I finished school to get married. This sounded good to me, but soon after telling Willie we would have to wait, it occurred to me: I could have Willie and a new car, too.

Pat said I was lucky to get him, for when a former girl friend, Tillie May, heard we were not getting married right away, she was really after him. Soon after we were married the car payment came due, and I realized why he had married me instead of Tillie May. I had a job and she didn't.

PAPA: NO COMIC STRIP HILLBILLY

Many people have mistaken images of how hill country people, or "hillbillies" as we are called, live. The image portrayed in comic books and other media are of a misguided nature. Some people are also led

Papa. Drawing by Willie Ledford.

to believe that hill people are ignorant. This stems from the fact that until recent years the people were scattered and schools were few and far between. The families were large and everyone, including the kids, had to work.

Papa's father died and left a big family. Papa was just a kid, but he had to quit school and work to keep food on the table. He only had a fifth grade education, but he was a very smart man. He kept a ledger book and records of all his farm business, and could figure cotton, corn, and cattle prices as well as any banker. He once worked an algebra problem for me. I couldn't work the problem, and Johnnie, the only one with enough education to help me, was nowhere to be found. Papa said, "Let me see the problem." After working it out, Mama said, "George, how did you ever do that?" He showed us his scratch sheet and said, "I just substituted cows and hogs for the X's and Y's, and it came out right."

Austin was bringing his born-and-raised "Dee-troit" bride to meet the family for the first time. He approached Papa to play the part of the stereotypical hillbilly. He wanted Papa to go down to the old Tucker shack, which was falling down, and sit on the porch with a jug in his hand and a shotgun by his side. "I don't think that's a good idea, son," Papa said. "We don't want that little gal thinking even for a minute that us Locks are so trifling we'd set around and let a house fall down around us."

"HEY THERE, PAPA"

Papa was not a tall man, only about five feet, five inches. He was overweight due to Mama's good cooking. If he had let his beard grow and worn a red suit, he could easily have passed for Santa Claus. He had a round belly that shook when he laughed like a bowl full of jelly, and he laughed often. Papa wore a Stetson felt hat, khaki pants, and Florsheim shoes.

When I think of Papa, my photographic mind always sees him with a mischievous look lurking behind his ever-present smile. He always had a joke to tell. The "Hey There" joke is one he often told while porch sitting:

A shy young man, while walking down the street, saw a beautiful young girl porch sitting. As he passed by he said, "Hey there." She smiled back and said, "Hey there." He said to himself, "She sure is pretty. I wonder if she's married? I'll walk around the block and try to see if she's wearing a wedding ring." As he approached her again, her hands were concealed, and he could not see if she were wearing a wedding ring, so he just said, "Hey there." She said, "Hey there." As he walked away he thought, "Darn, I should have come right out and asked if she's married. I'm going to try again." Around the block he went, and when he approached her, he again said, "Hey there." She said, "Hey there." He said, "Is your husband home?" She said, "Yes." He said, "Tell him I said, 'Hey there.'"

Kinda corny, huh? But when Papa told it, it was so funny.

Papa and the car.   *Debby and her dolls.*

When in his sixties, Papa developed emphysema, and after fighting the battle for several years, he lost. The family gathered at the funeral home for the first viewing of the body. When the curtains were drawn, and I realized Papa would never be home with us again, I felt I couldn't bear to go forward and see him lying dead in a casket.

As Mama stood looking lovingly down into Papa's face, she motioned to me, saying, "Come here, honey. It's okay. Papa's telling his 'Hey There' joke." As I looked at that dear face and saw the unmistakable, mischievous expression, I smiled. Papa could always make me smile, even when I was feeling my worst. I was convinced he was porch sitting in Heaven telling the "Hey There" joke.

OUR FIRSTBORN

The first Mother's Day after my marriage to Willie, Johnnie received a beautiful corsage of red carnations from her husband. The card read, "I hope someday you will be the mother of my children." It was so sweet that Johnnie cried, and I almost cried, too.

When I asked Willie why he hadn't gotten a corsage for me, he said, "Why should I get you anything for Mother's Day? You're no more a mother than I am. Why do people want kids anyhow? They're nothing but trouble." Well, giving a corsage wouldn't have broken his arm or anything. I could see right away it was going to be difficult having a sister whose husband was very thoughtful when mine wasn't; however, I guess it works both ways. I didn't get him anything for Father's Day, either. After all, he was no more a father than I.

After we had been married about a year, I got up one morning feeling awfully sick to my stomach. Never having felt this way before, I suspected I was pregnant. Willie kept saying it was only something I ate. After telling Johnnie of my suspicions she bought the cutest pair of little white booties with blue ribbons. She said, "If it's a girl we can get pink ribbons." She and I were having a great time oohing and aahing over the booties when Willie came in from work. When he saw the booties he said, "You haven't even been to the doctor yet—you may be counting your chickens before they hatch," and stalked out of the house. Johnnie and I laughed at him, for we knew it would hatch. She hatched all right, a beautiful little black-haired baby girl.

Willie fell so in love with that baby. The day we came home from the hospital he held her all day and half into the night. After I went back to work Willie could never understand why we had to pay someone to keep Debby. He thought they should be paying us. He now knew why people wanted children. We have two boys also, and love them equally as well, but our little girl, our firstborn, will always have a special place in our hearts.

GETTING AWAY FROM IT ALL

Soon after Debby was born the factory where Willie worked closed, and we were forced to move to the big city about eighty miles away from our hometown. Two children, many P.T.A meetings, and several camping vacations later, we began to long for the hassle-free days of our youth. While scanning the ads for a possible retirement getaway, this one caught our attention: "35 secluded acres in the beautiful hills of Tennessee. Some lake frontage." We loaded the kids in the car and headed east.

It was a three-hour drive to the real estate office. The land was about fifteen miles south of the office and the small town. We were tired and hungry, so the real estate man suggested a stop at the Dinner Bell Restaurant before our trip out to look over the land. The restaurant was a large building with a shake-shingle roof, and there were printed cottage curtains on the windows, a huge stone fireplace with iron pots sitting on the hearth, and iron skillets and an old-fashioned corn popper hanging nearby. It was too hot for a fire, but huge logs lay ready for a fire when needed.

A buffet was prepared consisting of chicken and dressing, green beans, creamed potatoes, slaw, homemade rolls and corn bread, with coffee or tea to drink. The meal was delicious; however, we felt very out of place. Everybody seemed to know everybody, and there was a lot of talking and visiting back and forth from table to table. Everyone who came in really gave us the once-over, knowing that we were strangers and didn't really belong.

After finishing our meal and being told, "Y'all come back, now," we took a tour of the town. The courthouse stood surrounded by one bank, a small grocery store, and one large so-called supermarket. One clothing store, a store called the Family Center (much like a dollar store), a barbershop, a flower shop, two beauty shops, a post office, a filling station, a funeral home, one red light, a high school, and a grammar school completed our tour. This was definitely a small town—just the escape for which we had been looking.

We went back to the real estate office. The man got into his car and said, "Follow me." After many hills and curves, and the feeling that we'd never get there, we finally arrived at our destination; it was strictly in the boonies. The road ended at the river and the property line. The river was the beautiful, sparkling Tennessee. At the back of the property was a large lake fed by the river. The man said the fishing was great, and we could actually see a fish jump up out of the water ever' so often. This really sold Willie and the two boys, but I was a bit apprehensive. The closest shopping mall was sixty-five miles away. How could I endure that?

Willie, the great talker when he wants to convince me of something, talked about what a good investment the land would be; also, it would be several years before we actually moved and we could have it paid for by then, and then he'd build me a beautiful house overlooking the lake. I gave in. We put ourselves in hock and bought the land.

After a summer of driving 150 miles with all our camping equipment, we decided it would be best to buy a house trailer, set it up on the main road so we could enjoy it now, and build our house later. Our neighbor, a hog farmer, said if we'd put it across the road up on the hill, he could look out his front window and keep an eye on it while we were away.

Willie and I were both working a lot of overtime at our jobs, and after two years had paid off the land. The changes that were taking place in the schools and where Willie worked, and the fact that Willie had planned to retire in a few years anyway, made us believe it would be best to go ahead and move. Our sixth grader could go to the small school nearby, where the threat of drugs and such had yet to spread. This decision to move earlier than planned put me in a trailer overlooking a hog pen instead of a house overlooking a lake...not quite the dream come true, but we'd manage. The house would come later.

A LEDFORD BY ANY
OTHER NAME...

Previously, all business pertaining to our property had been taken care of by mail. Our first trip into town—to start a bank account and get our voter registration changed to our new address—proved to be quite a confusing experience.

The steps going up to the beautiful old courthouse were worn. As we walked into the lobby there was a staircase to the right with beautifully carved banisters and spindles. The moldings and other trims were many, many years old and intricately carved. The walls were lined with large paintings and photos of mayors, sheriffs, and other town officials dating back to the 1800s. It was a hot day; there was no air-conditioning, the huge windows were raised, the office doors were open, and the people working had fans sitting on their desks.

We went into the first office on the left and asked where we should go to register to vote and get a license for the car. The man in charge said, "Who are you?"

Willie replied, "I'm Willie Ledford. We've just moved here and . . ."

"Oh, yeah, you're Willie Ledbetter's boy. You moving back here to stay?"

"No, no. I'm not Willie Ledbetter, I'm Willie Ledford."

"Willie who? How d'ya spell that? Where you from? Whose place did ya buy?"

After we answered all his questions, the man finally said, "I can fix ya up with a car license, but to register you'll have to go upstairs to the first office on your right."

The license taken care of, we proceeded upstairs. We walked in and said we just moved here and wanted to register to vote. The questions began again: "Who are you? Whose place did ya buy? What's the address there? How d'ya spell that name again?"

Willie said he'd go back to the car and wait for me if I wanted to check out the stores. He never liked shopping. I was walking down the street when an old lady stopped me and said, "Hon, who's in the funeral home?"

I said, "I beg your pardon."

She repeated, "Who's in the funeral home?"

"I don't know."

She then said, "Whose girl are you?"

After a puzzled moment, I finally realized she was asking who my father was. I said, "I don't think you would know my father."

She said, "Well, who are you, hon?"

"I'm Ibbie Ledford."

"Oh, you married Willie Ledbetter's boy, didn't ya? Are y'all moving back home?" It took a while, but I finally explained who I was, where I came from, that we bought the old Denton place, how many children we had, and how long we'd been married; also, where I grew up and why we didn't buy a place there and why we were moving here when we had no kin living here. I'd begun to wonder why we'd moved here myself.

When I got back to the car, Willie asked me what I thought of the stores in town. I explained that I never got to the stores and what a third degree I had gotten from a woman on the street. When he asked who she was, to my amazement I didn't even know her name. She was so busy asking me questions and I answering them that I never thought of asking.

I was ready to go home, but Willie said we needed to go to the bank. To our surprise, we were greeted with friendliness and efficiency. The president of the bank met us with a handshake and a friendly smile. He knew all about us, the place we had bought, where we were from, and even how to spell our name. You see, the real estate man was a good friend of his. Our business completed, we felt we must make one more stop at the farmers' co-op to buy grass seed.

After asking for lawn seed, the man said, "What kind ya want?" Willie explained he didn't know what kind was needed for this area or how much seed he'd need. "How big a yard ya got?" He got the kind of seed we'd need and the amount needed for the area we had to sow. "How ya gonna sow it? You got a spreader?"

Willie said, "No, I was just going to sow it by hand."

"I got a spreader here," the man said, but Willie told him he hated to buy one for just this one job.

"You don't have to buy it. I'm a-loaning it to ya."

So we paid for the seed, took the spreader, and started to leave. Then Willie said, "By the way, don't you want my name and address?"

The man said, "You're goin' to bring it back, ain't ya? Then there's no need to write down ye name and address. Besides, I know who ya are and where ya live. You bought the old Denton place, didn't ya?"

As we started out, while pausing at the seed display, we overheard another man asking, "Who was that?"

The man said, "That's Willie Ledbetter's boy. He bought the old Denton place."

LIVING OFF THE LAND

We had great plans. We'd get a cow. I learned to milk while growing up on a farm and could still remember the great taste of hand-churned butter. And chickens! We'd get chickens, too; it'd be such fun to "pick the eggs," as our city son said he wanted to do. And we definitely wanted to grow our own vegetables. Yes, we were gonna live off the land.

We were itching to get started on our garden. Our neighbor plowed up the garden spot with his big tractor, but if we were going to have a good garden, we'd need some of our own tools. We bought a tiller, hoe, rake, and shovel. Quite a bit of money was invested here, but we'd be using these tools for many years.

I had been reading up on organic gardening. We found an old barn where we could get manure and a place where there was once an old sawmill. We hauled manure and rotted sawdust by the truckloads and worked it into the soil. We were working from sunup to sundown, but the fresh vegetables surely would reward us for the hard work. However, it didn't turn out quite the way we anticipated.

The sweet peas were up about two inches. I was so proud of them. Overnight the rabbits ate three rows right down to the ground. We set out tomato plants. In a few days the cutworms started on them, and the plants that survived got tomato worms. We picked the worms off and used them for fish bait; there were very few tomatoes to eat, but at least we caught a mess of catfish with the worms. The beans were blooming—looked like we might have a few messes of beans. We went out one morning and a swarm of some kind of bug had all the plants in the garden covered. They were even eating the marigolds and nasturtiums the book said to plant to ward off insects.

We have since learned that our rocky soil requires chemical fertil-izer—as well as hard work—to produce, and we have had some good gardens. We have also learned there is always an abundance of fresh vegetables in our area for sale cheaper than we can raise them. We never got around to the chickens and the cow. Living off the land wasn't as easy as it seemed to be when we were kids. So, selling off all our land appeared to be the answer. We found our dream house already built overlooking a lake, and have really retired.

Willie fishes and I write, piece quilts, and cook. It gets a little too quiet here at times, and I long for the city and dream of how wonderful it would be to sink my teeth into a Big Mac, go to a shopping mall without driving for an hour and a half, have coffee with the neighbors, and be near my grandchildren. I also think of the traffic, and hustle and bustle that goes with the city, and I truly don't know if I'd like living there again. I have my dream house and my dream of a husband, and he won't budge, so I guess I'll remain a country girl for the rest of my life.

Willie Ledford on the lake in front of our home.

NOT ALWAYS THE CHARM
THAT COUNTS

For her twenty-fifth anniversary Johnnie received a gold charm bracelet. The charm had the beautiful Robert Browning quote imprinted on it, "Grow Old With Me, The Best Is Yet To Be." Johnnie and I really had a good ball over that charm bracelet.

When Willie saw it, I asked if he were getting one for me for our twenty-fifth. He said, "You've already had the best," to which I replied, "Are you saying this is it? This is as good as it's going to get? If that's all there is then bring on the booze."

"Just kidding, honey, just kidding. It's been great. Those unforgettable vacations on the lake. The breezy damp tent we had to sleep in. The wonderful feeling of sand sifting through my toes, and that was after I went to bed at night. The gourmet meals prepared on a smoky camp stove or an open fire by an excellent outdoor chef, me. A bathroom within easy walking distance, and we didn't even have to flush. The moonlit nights sitting around a campfire, swatting mosquitoes, grabbing a kid by the shirttail just in time to save him from falling into the fire. Swimming, skiing, pitching washers, playing ball, fishing, and other family fun.

"Remember Old Blue, the big blue catfish we caught jug fishing? We tied him out in the lake and showed him to everyone who came by. We had intended to eat him on our last day at camp, but took a vote and decided to have sandwiches for lunch, and let Old Blue go. We would come home with enough sand in our shoes, car, and bedding to make our own beach. We'd also come home with beautifully tanned children, with stories of Old Blue and other adventures."

Many anniversaries have passed and I still don't have a gold charm bracelet; it's now just me and you, kid. The big house is lonely at times. We've had our battles. I've won some and lost some. Willie has taken a lot a lip from me. He has never hit me, but he got so mad at me one time he hit the wall and made a hole in the Sheetrock. I kinda watched it after that; I surmised there may not always be a wall handy, and I could end up with a hole in my head.

As far as I know, Willie has been faithful to me all these years, but husbands are like children: you can't watch them all the time. There's been a lot of water and a lot of cars over the bridge since we first met, and the road has been bumpy at times, but I'm glad we stuck it out, glad he's the father of my children and his kids and my kids are our kids, and that he is the one I'm growing old with. I may just go out and buy that charm bracelet for myself on our next anniversary. The inscription will read: "We've made it this far, why not all the way."

"YAWL COME TO SEE US WHEN YE KIN"

Hillbillies are as well educated these days as people in other areas of the country and have the ability to speak the English language correctly; however, among themselves they speak a language all their own. Any hillbilly who moves away, develops a more correct way of speaking, and loses some of his or her accent may be accused of putting on "airs" or being "uppity." The scene in this story is the Tennessee hills. Some old friends get together and this is the conversation that could occur. Keep in mind while reading this story that the incorrect spelling reflects the accent of the conversation. Just pronounce the words as written and you will be speaking like a true hillbilly.

"Well, lookie here! It's Peggy Jo and J. T. Yawl come on in the house an' git ya a cheer. Yawl're sure a sight fer sore eyes. Seems like yairs since we seen ya last. How many ars did it take yawl to git cheer?"

"'Bout two ars. Had a bitta trouble with the battry. Hit took out on us. A feller lent me a wranch. Soon's I tightened up the cables she hit right off. I took back the wranch, said, 'Muchablidge,' and we wuz back on the road agin in no time flat. Skeered we'd have tar trouble. Mah old tars are sorta wore thin. We shore wuz glad when we made the tarn into yawlses road."

"How come yawl ain't been to see us fer such a long spell?"

"Well, yawl know how tis. We got to keep the youngins in school so's they kin get their larning. Thar's plowin' to do and crops to put in. Come July we got all them veg'tables to put up. The cows has gotta be milked twiced a day. Thar's the hogs and chickens to feed and eiggs to gather. Seems like work ain't never done on the farm. Some uv our kin is taking keer uv the place whilst we're gone, but I got me a idy we better not stay too long. They might be kinfolk, but they won't take keer of the place like we do."

"You youngins go outdoors and play and don't be a-gitten in the crick. If ye git all wet and muddy you're lible to gitta whuppin. Us menfolk is gonna set out cheer on the porch and jaw a bit whilst you womenfolk cook up some grub."

"Nice swang ya got cheer, Billy Ray."

"Yep, me and Ida May, we come out cheer on a Sunday when the weather's purdy and swang and swang and swang."

"I never keered much fer swanging. Kinda makes me feel sickish."

"How's yore youngins been, J. T.?"

"Junior, he had pneumonie back in the winter and wuz purdy bad off fer a spell, but he's might nigh good as new agin now. I wuz under the weather thar fer a spell, but I perked right up come sprang."

"Whatchya been up to, you old hound dog, you?"

"Not much a nothin', you old hound dog. Whatchya been up to?"

"Well, me and the missus got us a idy to go in the resternt bidness, but the bank won't give us no loan. They got shedda Bruce, Jr.; said they couldn't run a bank no more the way him and his daddy afore him run it. Most of their deals wuz made with just a handshake. Bruce, Jr., shore has a good tarn. Them gitten shed of him has almost ruint that bank. Hardly nobody goes in thar no more. Them high-falutin' college-educated bankers jest don't know how to handle people in these here parts.

"We wuz gonna have a resternt whar people could git a good stick-to-the-ribs meal without costing them a arm and a laig. If folks ever got a taste of Ida May's cookin', they'd bag fer more. It wuz gonna be built ovair on top uv the hill. We still aim to save up and do it without no help from nobody.

"How's fishin' up in yore parts, J. T.?"

"Fair to middlin'. Yep, I'd say fair to middlin'. The crappie ain't bit this year like they usual do; been too hot. The water's gotta cool down afore you kin ketch many crappie. But my boy thar did ketch a bass that wuz a whopper. Weighed pert'ner ten pounds. I don't recollect us ever havin' a summer as hot as this'n or a winter as warm as the last'n. Lotsa days wudn't no need to build a far."

"I hear tell thar's a big deemand fer cotton now."

"Yep, come next yair I'm a-fixin' to put in close ta hunnert acres more cotton. Price is likely to go sky high. For a while now thar ain't been much call fer cotton. The feller who come up with a piece of goods that don't have to be arned really put a cramp in the cotton bidness. But now the tide's tarned. Young folks is goin' hog-wild over cotton duds. I seen a little gal on TV, one uv them whatchya call rock stars. Now she woulda wore 'bout a size ten, but she musta had on her daddy's coat, 'cause it wuz way yonder too big fer her. Her britches fit mighty good though. The coat and britches wuz all faded and had ravelly holes all in 'em, and they hadn't even been arned. Mama woulda never let us wear sumpin' like 'at to the cotton patch, much less in public. Sometimes we had to wear patched britches, but Mama could sew on a patch that'd take a spyglass to see it. Now they sell 'em right outta the stores with patches they aim to show; even use different colors to what the britches is. Some even got holes all in 'em with no thought ta patchin'. I 'lowed as how them advertizers was brainwashin' folks into buyin' the likes of that and callin' it high fashion."

"Dude said, 'Folks that'd pay good money fer them rags ain't got no brains to wash.' Well, me and Old Dude is shore with one another on that."

"You menfolk come on in the house. Supper's on the table. Youngins! Mary Jo, Steven Lyn, Matty Pearl, John Franklyn, yawl come on in and git washed up fer supper. You menfolk quit yore jawin' and git to the supper table 'fore we throw it out now. Matty Pearl, it's yore tarn to say grace."

"God is great, God is good, and we thank Him for this food. Amen!"

"Peggy Jo, you and J. T. just take out and hep yourselves now. Thar's fried chicken, mashed taters, and gravy. Wait till ya taste Ida May's chicken gravy."

"I got 'nanner puddin' for dessert, so yawl save some room fer that."

"Yawl needn't hurry off, now."

"We gotta go, but we shore have got our enjoys outta this visit. Hurry up, youngins, and git yore rags on. We're a-fixin' to leave directly."

"Yawl take keer goin' home and come back now, ye hear?"

"WHAT DID YOU PLAY WITH WHEN YOU WERE A LITTLE GIRL, GRANNY?"

I tell my granddaughter Deidra that pretend games were the most fun. When I made a playhouse, it was not really a house but a place under the big oak tree with rooms carefully marked off by sticks. Cardboard boxes were our tables and rocks our chairs. Mama let me use some of her jar lids for plates, and my knives and forks were sticks. I made mud pies and cakes, using grass for coconut. A stick horse was tied to a nearby tree. Unlike Deidra's spring horse, my stick horse would buck and jump and run down the road leaving a cloud of dust behind.

We swung on grapevines, played hide-and-seek, London Bridge, drop-the-handkerchief, kick-the-can, Annie-Over, wave me out of jail, sling tail, deck ball, jump rope, jacks, and hopscotch. My favorite doll was the one Mama made for me. It was made out of a flour sack, with embroidered eyes and mouth and yellow yarn for hair. She was dressed in a beautiful blue and white polka-dot dress and bonnet and her shoes were made of shiny white oilcloth. I named her Jenny. She was my constant companion.

Another doll I cherished was the one I received as a gift from Aunt Ibbie and Uncle John. Her body was cloth, but her arms, legs, and head were china. She had on a long white dress and bonnet trimmed with lace and ribbons. She was a beautiful doll, almost too pretty to play with. I named her Emily because Emily was Aunt Ibbie's middle name. Ten years old, and thinking I was getting too old to play with dolls, I tied a ribbon under Jenny's and Emily's arms and hung them on the wall out of reach of my little nieces.

"Do you still have Jenny and Emily, Granny?" Deidra asked me.

Uncle John and Hickernut and Walnut.

"No, Deidra, I gave them away."

It was Christmas, times were hard, and there was no money to buy dolls for Margaret's two little girls. Mama said I must not be selfish. I must give the dolls to my little nieces. I kissed Jenny and Emily goodbye and gave them to Margaret to put under the Christmas tree. Cherry and Eva were too young to appreciate and take care of the dolls. One day I found Emily outside. Her beautiful dress and bonnet were nowhere to be seen, and one arm was missing. I don't know what happened to Jenny. Even though I was twelve years old and too big to play with dolls, I cried like a baby. I really loved those dolls.

Cousin Nellie and I spent many hours playing paper dolls. Betsy McCall was my favorite. The dolls had glamorous clothes and we played with them much like Deidra plays with her Barbie dolls, only these dolls and clothes were made of paper.

Jacks was my favorite game. I soon learned, after Papa stepped on one with his bare foot, not to leave my jacks on the floor. If my dress didn't have a pocket (little girls wore dresses all the time in those days), I carried them around in my hand most all the time, earning me the nickname "Jack." I could go all the way to tens without touching, put them in the basket, remove them one by one, line them up and jump each jack over the other, then pick them all up for the end of the game. I was jacks champion of the whole Millsfield school. Nobody could beat me. Sometimes Mrs. Florence would clear her desk and let us play on it. It was the best place, for the desk was made of solid oak and caused the jack ball to bounce real high.

I don't remember when I finally let go of those jacks, or where I put them. I bought jacks and paper dolls for Deidra, but she doesn't seem to enjoy them. Jacks and paper dolls and the other games we enjoyed so much were part of another generation and just can't compete with today's video games and TV, but my friends and relatives still remember the good times we had, and some still call me Jack.

DOWN MEMORY LANE

My three sisters and I went back to the rural community where we were born, something we had been planning to do for years. As we turned off the main highway we truly began our trip down memory lane.

Everything looked so different. The old house where the Tickles lived had been remodeled and stood tall and proud. A little farther down the lane was the old church house—the doors off, weeds grown up, a fence around it with a lock on the gate. As we pulled over I noticed a no trespassing sign. Johnnie said, "Oh, surely that doesn't mean us." We walked around back, but there was no way in there. We then proceeded around the side where we hoped to find a gate. Margaret lagged behind, seeking a way in. About the time Johnnie, Irene, and I reached the locked gate, Marg yelled, "I'm in."

"Start the singing," I called. "We'll be there directly." She began to sing "I'll Fly Away." We all joined in as we climbed over the locked gate, hoping the people in the house across the road were watching TV instead of us.

As we entered the old church a quietness fell upon us, each one reminiscing in her own mind of the olden times. The inside had evidently been used as storage for hay, for loose hay littered the floor.

The stage was still there along with the side railing. I would have given my dentures for that railing to go in my home. It was coming loose and could easily have been pulled up and carted out. Although it probably meant nothing to anyone else and would just rot away, to take it would have been stealing from what I still considered the house of the Lord. We'd be lucky if we got out of there without being arrested for trespassing or lunacy. I was glad the old church was still standing and I could visit it once more. It may not be there the next time I come, and if it is I may be too old to climb over the gate.

As we continued down the lane we went over a rise that I remembered as being a steep hill when we walked up it to school. They must have grated it down. We were nearing Grandmama and Grandpapa Lane's old place. Aunt Ibbie and Uncle John lived there after the "Grands" died. There was nothing there; the house, the barn, everything was gone, with no sign that anyone had once lived there. I wondered if we could find a sprig or a bud of some flower that used

The old homeplace. Drawing by Willie Ledford.

to grow in the yard and was tended so lovingly by Aunt Ibbie. Would the cool spring where the drinking water came from, and where Grandmama kept her milk and butter cold, still be there? It would have meant a walk through a lot of brush to find out, so we decided not to get out of the car. We just sat there in silence for a moment letting our memories kick in.

We came to an open field with a small sycamore tree—the only tree left standing—at the edge. A beer can someone had been using for target practice hung from a limb. "This is where our house stood," Irene said. "It couldn't be," I declared. "Where are the large oak trees and the orchard?" I could see some trees a little farther down the lane. That must be the place! The road became impassable, so we got out of the car and began to walk. When we got to the trees they were growing in a fencerow. Irene had been right: there was nothing left at the old homeplace but a sycamore tree with a beer can hanging on a limb. We wandered around the field searching for remains of our childhood memories. Finding only a piece of broken china, we turned around and headed back up the lane.

The old schoolhouse was still standing, but the doors and windows were out and the floor and roof were caving in. A little farther along we stopped at the brick church that has replaced the old one to see what time service started on Sunday. We planned to attend. A stop at the graveyard and Uncle Sam's store completed our day.

As long as I have my memories I can still jump rope in the schoolyard; hear the singing in the old church; sit on the porch swing; climb the apple trees in the orchard, sit on a limb, and eat apples; and lie in the hayloft of the old barn and dream of the future. Memories are one of the most wonderful things God gave us. At the beginning of this book I thanked Mama and Papa for the memories they helped me to create. Now I must thank God for the ability to retain those memories and pray that He will allow me to retain them for the rest of my life here on earth.

Soups and Salads

A country scene near our home.

BROCCOLI SOUP

1 pkg. (10 oz.) frozen chopped
   broccoli
¼ cup butter
¼ cup self-rising flour
2 cups chicken broth
2 cups milk
2 tsp. onion flakes
½ cup chopped Velveeta cheese
½ cup cream

Cook broccoli according to directions on package. Set aside. In heavy saucepan over medium heat, melt butter. Add flour and cook 2 minutes. Stir in chicken broth, milk, and onion. Continue cooking and stirring until mixture begins to thicken. Add broccoli, cheese, and cream. Stir until cheese melts, but do not let boil. Remove from heat. Serve as is, or put in blender for a smoother soup. Serves 6.

POTATO SOUP

4 medium potatoes, cubed
1 qt. water
1 tsp. salt
¼ tsp. pepper
2 tbsp. fried meat grease
4 slices bacon, fried and crumbled

Cook potatoes in boiling water 15 minutes. Add salt, pepper, and meat grease. Cook 10 minutes longer. Remove from heat. Mash potatoes lightly with fork. Serve in bowls and sprinkle bacon on top. Serves 4.

DISHWATER SOUP

I would not suggest you try this recipe. It probably isn't very good, even after adding salt.

Put white beans in iron pot. Cover with water. Set on stove over high heat. Go out to work in garden and forget beans. When you return to the kitchen, beans will be badly burned. Dump all beans out of pot except those stuck to bottom. After washing dishes, pour dishpan full of dirty greasy water in bean pot. Put on back of stove to soak.

Mama had been working feverishly all day trying to get the garden planted before the rains came. She had not had time to prepare any snack for that day. Top, Chock, and Austin came in from school looking for a snack. There were no tea cakes on the table, no fried pies in the pie safe, no meat and biscuits in the warming closet. Chock said, "Maybe there's something in here," lifting the lid on the pot on back of the stove. "Looks like soup."

"What kind?" Top asked.

"I see some beans in it," Chock said as he stirred it with a spoon and took a taste. "It's not very good."

"Let me have a taste," Top said. "Not bad. You get some bowls. I think all it needs is some salt."

Top was stirring and adding salt to the dishwater soup when Mama came into the kitchen. "What in the world are you boys doing? Do you know you were about to eat burnt beans and dishwater? I declare, you boys would eat anything. If you'll clear out of my kitchen, I'll have a batch of tea cakes made in about thirty minutes."

"Could you make that fifteen minutes, Mama?" Top asked. "And I think the dishwater soup would have been pretty good after I added the salt."

DUCK SOUP

1 small duck
6 cups water, or enough to cover
   duck
1 tsp. salt
½ cup chopped onion
½ cup chopped celery
1 cup raw rice
¼ tsp. black pepper
½ cup water
1 tbsp. flour

Put duck in pot. Add water and salt. Cover pot and boil until duck is tender, about 1   hours. Remove duck from pot. Set aside to cool. Measure broth, adding water if necessary to make 5 cups. Add onion, celery, rice, and black pepper to broth. Cover pot and boil 20 minutes. Debone duck, discarding bone and skin. Chop duck and add to broth. Mix   cup water with the flour until smooth. Add to broth. Stir and let come to boil. Remove from heat and serve hot. Serves 6 to 8.

TOMATO SOUP AND DUMPLINGS

1 can (10½ oz.) cream of tomato
   soup
1 cup water
1 tsp. dried onion flakes
½ tsp. dried basil leaves
⅛ tsp. black pepper

Mix all ingredients together in heavy 2-quart saucepan. Heat slowly to boiling point while preparing dumplings.

DUMPLINGS

1½ cups biscuit baking mix
¾ cup grated American cheese
⅓ cup evaporated milk
⅓ cup water

Mix all ingredients together. Drop by teaspoons into boiling soup. Cover pan and boil slowly 15 minutes. Remove dumplings to serving bowls. Pour soup over. Serves 4.

SOUP MIX

Mama "put up" many quarts of soup mix every year. It was good as is, or meat and other vegetables could be added. When I prepare the mix I freeze it instead of canning it.

2 qt. fresh purple hull peas
2 qt. fresh butter beans or lima
  beans
Water to cover
1 qt. fresh corn cut from the cob
4 lb. fresh tomatoes, peeled and
  chopped
2 tsp. salt

Place peas and beans in large stew pot. Cover with water and bring to a boil. Boil 15 minutes, checking from time to time to see if more water is needed. Mix in corn, tomatoes, and salt. Bring to a boil and cook 15 minutes more. Cool. Spoon into freezer containers.

When ready to serve, thaw and place in saucepan. Add 1 tablespoon fried meat grease, 1 tablespoon butter, and more water if needed. Taste, adding more salt and black pepper if needed. Serve with corn bread or crackers.

GARDEN-FRESH GREEN PEA SOUP

2 cups fresh green peas
1 can (10¾ oz.) chicken broth
1 cup water
½ cup chopped onion
1 tsp. salt, or to taste
¼ tsp. pepper
½ cup half-and-half

Place peas, chicken broth, water, onion, and salt in heavy saucepan. Cook over medium heat about 20 minutes. Add more water if needed while cooking. Process peas in blender until smooth. Add pepper and half-and-half. Return to low heat until heated through, but do not boil. Serves 6.

HE-MAN SALAD

1 pkg. (8 oz.) elbow macaroni
¾ cup mayonnaise
¼ cup sweet pickle relish
¼ tsp. salt
1 can (12 oz.) corned beef,
   chopped
1 can (17 oz.) green peas, drained
1 cup cubed Swiss cheese
½ cup chopped celery

Cook macaroni according to directions on package. Drain. Rinse in cold water. Place in bowl. Add remaining ingredients. Toss lightly to mix. Chill until ready to serve. Serves 10.

CUCUMBER AND ONIONS

1 large cucumber
1 large onion
1 tsp. salt
1 cup white vinegar
¼ tsp. black pepper

Peel and slice cucumber and onion. Sprinkle with salt. Pour vinegar over all. Cover and refrigerate several hours or overnight. Drain. Place on serving dish and sprinkle with black pepper. Serves 8 to 10.

DEBBY'S NACHO MAIN DISH SALAD

1 lb. ground beef
1 cup chopped onion
1 can (16 oz.) red kidney beans, drained
½ lb. chopped cheese, cheddar or your choice
1 cup Catalina salad dressing
1 bag (6 oz.) nacho chips
2 cups shredded lettuce

In skillet over medium heat, brown ground beef and onions, stirring to break up beef as it browns. Drain off grease. Add beans, cheese, and dressing to beef. Put half of nacho chips in bowl. Spoon half of ground beef mixture on top of nachos. Put half of lettuce on top of this. Repeat layers. Serve while hot. Serves 12.

POTATO SALAD

5 cups cubed cooked potatoes,
  about 6 medium
2 boiled eggs, peeled and chopped
1 cup chopped onion
1 cup chopped celery
½ cup chopped dill pickle
½ tsp. salt, or to taste
¼ tsp. pepper
⅓ cup sweet pickle relish
1 tbsp. mustard
1 cup mayonnaise
Lettuce
Paprika

In large bowl, mix together potatoes, eggs, onion, celery, dill pickle, and salt and pepper. In small bowl, mix together sweet pickle relish, mustard, and mayonnaise. Pour over potatoes. Toss together to mix. Line salad bowl with lettuce. Spoon potato salad over lettuce. Sprinkle top with paprika. Serves 8.

WILTED LETTUCE SALAD

Leaf lettuce
Green onions
Radishes
6 slices bacon or middling meat
¼ cup vinegar

In large bowl, cut lettuce, green onions, and radishes. Cut meat into small pieces. Fry meat in skillet till brown. Remove from skillet. Add vinegar to hot grease. Pour over greens. Toss lightly. Sprinkle chopped meat over top.

KRAUT SLAW

2 cans (1 lb.) kraut
½ cup chopped green pepper
½ cup chopped green onion
½ cup diced celery
¾ cup sugar
3 tbsp. white vinegar
¼ tsp. black pepper

Drain and squeeze juice from kraut. Add all other ingredients to kraut and mix well. Cover and refrigerate. This slaw will keep a week or more if kept refrigerated. Great with fish. Serves 8.

SLAW

3 cups chopped cabbage
½ cup chopped onion
¼ tsp. salt
¼ tsp. black pepper
½ cup mayonnaise
1 tsp. mustard
2 tbsp. sweet pickle juice from jar
of sweet pickles

Mix together cabbage, onion, salt, and pepper. Mix mayonnaise, mustard, and pickle juice. Pour over cabbage and mix well. Good with fish. Serves 6.

ANOTHER SLAW

3 cups chopped cabbage
1 tomato, chopped
½ cup chopped green onion
½ tsp. salt
½ cup mayonnaise

Mix all together. Good with beans and corn bread. Serves 6.

SWEET AND SOUR SLAW

1 cabbage head
4 carrots
1 green pepper
⅔ cup sugar
1 cup vinegar

Shred cabbage. Scrape carrots and shred. Seed and chop green pepper. Mix all together in large bowl. In saucepan, mix sugar and vinegar together. Bring to a boil. Cool completely. Pour over cabbage mixture. Refrigerate until ready to serve. Serves 10.

Meats and Main Dishes

My nephew George Allen Lock going hunting.

A dog and his master.

BAKED QUAIL

6 quail
Salt and pepper
6 slices bacon
½ lb. mushrooms, sliced
1 cup chopped green onions
3 tbsp. butter or margarine

Wash quail well. Sprinkle with salt and pepper. Wrap each with bacon. Place in baking pan. Sauté mushrooms and onions in butter. Pour over quail. Put foil over all. Bake in 350-degree oven for 1 hour, or until quail are tender.

CHICKEN AND BREAD CASSEROLE

10 slices bread
2 cups chopped cooked chicken
1 cup chopped celery
2 cups shredded cheddar cheese
1 cup mayonnaise
2 eggs, beaten
½ tsp. salt
1½ cups milk

Trim crusts from bread, reserving crusts. Cut bread slices into diagonal quarters. Cut crusts into cubes. Mix together cubes, chicken, celery, and 1½ cups cheese. Spoon into 13-by-9-inch baking pan. Arrange bread quarters over chicken mixture.

Mix together mayonnaise, eggs, and salt. Gradually stir in milk to blend. Pour over bread. Sprinkle with remaining cheese. At this point you may cover and let set in refrigerator several hours or overnight. Bake uncovered in 350-degree oven for 30 to 40 minutes, until brown and bubbly. Serves 12.

CHICKALIN AND DUMPALINS

My children love this dish and gave it this name.

1 chicken, about 3 lb.
Water to cover
1 tsp. salt
2 cups diced potatoes
2 tsp. dried onion flakes
¼ tsp. black pepper

Wash chicken. Put into large pot with enough water to cover chicken. Add salt. Cover pot and cook on medium heat till chicken is tender, about 1 hour. Remove chicken from pot to cool. Add potatoes, onion flakes, and pepper to broth. May need to add more water at this time to make about 2 quarts of broth. Cover pot and cook 15 minutes.

Remove bones and skin from chicken and return chicken to pot. Make thickener of 1 cup cold water and 2 tablespoons flour. Beat with fork until smooth and stir into broth. Taste and add more salt, if needed. Drop in dumplings. Cover and simmer 15 minutes.

DUMPLINGS

½ cup water
4 tbsp. butter or margarine
⅔ cup self-rising flour
2 eggs, beaten

Bring water and butter to a boil. Remove from heat and add flour. Cool. Add eggs one at a time, beating until smooth. Drop by teaspoonfuls into simmering chicken broth. Serves 8 generously.

CHICKEN AND DRESSING WITH GIBLET GRAVY

1 stewing chicken, 3 lb. or more
6 cups water
1 tsp. salt
3 tbsp. butter or margarine
1 cup chopped celery
1 cup chopped onions
6 cups corn bread crumbs
4 cups stale bread crumbs
4 cups hot chicken broth, or
   enough to make mushy mixture
4 eggs, beaten
½ tsp. black pepper
¼ tsp. cayenne pepper
1 tsp. salt, or to taste
1 tbsp. sage

Wash chicken. Place in large pot. Add water and 1 tsp. salt. Bring to a boil. Cover pot and turn heat down. Cook 1 hour, adding more water if needed while chicken is cooking. Remove from broth to cool. Make dressing. Melt butter in skillet. Add celery and onions. Cook until tender. Put crumbs in large mixing bowl. Add chicken broth to make mixture like mush. Stir in celery, onions, eggs, and seasonings. Taste to see if more salt is needed. Pour into a 13-by-9-inch baking pan. Remove bones and skin from chicken. Place on top of dressing. Cover with foil. Bake in 400-degree oven for 45 minutes. Serves 12.

GIBLET GRAVY

Neck, gizzard, and liver of fowl
1 qt. water
⅓ cup self-rising flour
1 cup cold water
1 tsp. salt, or to taste
⅛ tsp. pepper
2 tsp. dried onion flakes
2 boiled eggs, peeled

Cook giblets in large saucepan with 1 qt. water for about 1 hour, until tender. Remove from broth and dice, pulling meat from neck bone. Add more water, if needed, to make 4 cups broth. Return giblets to broth. Blend flour with 1 cup water until smooth. Add to broth. Stir in salt, pepper, and onion flakes. Grate boiled eggs into broth. Cook 15 minutes longer. Good spooned over dressing.

SOUTHERN FRIED CHICKEN

1 frying-sized chicken
Water to cover
1 tbsp. salt
Cooking oil or shortening
2 cups self-rising flour

Put fryer pieces in large pan with enough water to cover chicken. Add salt and stir to dissolve salt. Let chicken remain in water while preparing to cook. Cover bottom of Dutch oven or frying pan with about 2 inches of cooking oil or shortening. Remove chicken from water 1 piece at a time and dredge in flour. Have oil hot. Drop in chicken. Turn heat down. Put lid on pan. Turn to brown on both sides, 8 to 10 minutes per side. Serves 6.

CHICKEN POT PIE

2 cups peeled, chopped potatoes
1 cup chopped celery
½ cup chopped onion
1 cup sliced carrots
Water to cover
1 tsp. salt
1 can (15 oz.) green peas, drained
2 cups chicken broth or leftover
   giblet gravy
2 cups chopped cooked chicken
¼ tsp. black pepper
Pie crust

Place potatoes, celery, onion, and carrots in saucepan. Cover with water. Add salt. Boil until tender, about 15 minutes. Remove from heat and drain. If chicken broth is thin, thicken with 2 tablespoons flour beaten into broth until smooth.

Mix vegetables, broth or gravy, chicken, and pepper together. Pour into 10-inch pie pan or 9-by-9-inch square pan. Cover top with pie crust. Bake in 350-degree oven for 45 minutes, or until crust is brown. For a quickie pie, substitute two 15-ounce cans mixed vegetables and 1 can cream of chicken soup for fresh vegetables and chicken broth. Serves 6 generously.

GRAVEDIGGERS' STEW

There was a time when graves were dug with picks and shovels by friends and neighbors of the deceased.

Mrs. Minnie Vaughn lived just down the road a piece from the graveyard; therefore, she felt it was her duty to put a hearty meal on the table for the gravediggers. She often served this stew. She gave me the recipe using her home-canned vegetables. Store-bought canned vegetables may be substituted.

1 stewing chicken
Water to cover
2 tsp. salt
¼ tsp. black pepper
2 cups chopped potatoes
1 cup chopped onions
1 qt. lima beans
1 pt. corn
1 qt. canned tomatoes, chopped

Place chicken in large pot. Cover with water. Add salt and pepper. Let boil at least 1 hour, or until chicken is tender. Remove from broth and remove skin and bones. Skim off fat from broth. If left to sit until cold, fat will be easily removed. Place broth back on stove, adding more water if needed to make 2 quarts. Add vegetables. Let come to a boil. Simmer 20 minutes. Add chicken pieces. Make thickener of 3 tablespoons flour and 1 cup water. Stir into simmering stew. Taste and add more salt if needed. Serve with corn bread. Serves 10.

CORNMEAL MUSH CAKES

1 cup self-rising cornmeal
1 cup cold water
2 cups boiling water
2 tbsp. melted butter or
    margarine

Mix meal and cold water together. Add boiling water. Cook in heavy saucepan until thick, stirring constantly, about 8 minutes. Pour into buttered loaf pan. Let cool, then cover and refrigerate overnight. Run knife around sides and remove from pan. Slice and fry in butter. Serve with butter and syrup. Makes 8 1-inch thick cakes.

BAKED CHEESE GRITS

6 cups water
1 tsp. salt
1½ cups regular grits
½ cup butter or margarine
½ lb. Velveeta cheese, chopped
3 eggs, beaten
Crumbled bacon

In heavy saucepan, bring water and salt to a boil. Gradually add grits, stirring constantly. Reduce heat. Cover and cook 10 minutes. Add butter and cheese, stirring till melted. Add beaten eggs. Pour into a greased baking dish. Bake in 350-degree oven for 45 minutes. Garnish with crumbled bacon. Good served for breakfast with gravy and eggs. Serves 8 to 10.

SAUSAGE AND CHEESE GRITS

1 lb. pork sausage
3 cups hot cooked grits
2 cups grated cheddar cheese
3 tbsp. butter or margarine,
  melted
3 eggs, beaten
1½ cups milk
½ cup grated parmesan cheese

In skillet, cook sausage until brown, stirring to break apart as it cooks. Drain. Spread into lightly greased 13-by-9-inch baking pan. Combine grits, cheddar cheese, and butter. Add eggs and milk. Pour over sausage. Sprinkle parmesan cheese over top. Bake in 350-degree oven for 1 hour, or until set and lightly brown. Serves 10 to 12.

OMELET

2 eggs
2 tbsp. water
Pinch of salt
Pinch of pepper
1 tbsp. butter or margarine

Beat together eggs, water, salt, and pepper. Add butter to a hot skillet. When melted, pour in eggs. Tilt pan so eggs go all over pan. Keep lifting and tilting pan until eggs no longer run. Fold in half. With spatula, lift out on serving platter. Before folding, one or more of these fillings may be added: cooked sausage, bacon, ham, cheese, onion, green pepper, or mushrooms. Serves 1.

BEEF STEW

1 lb. stew meat
Meat tenderizer
1 cup self-rising flour
2 tbsp. margarine
1 qt. water
1 envelope dry onion soup mix
3 cups cubed potatoes
2 cups sliced carrots

Sprinkle meat with tenderizer. Dredge in flour. Place margarine in Dutch oven to melt. Add meat and brown on all sides. Add water and soup mix. Simmer 30 minutes, adding more water if needed. Stir in potatoes and carrots. Cook additional 20 to 30 minutes, until meat and vegetables are tender. Serves 4 to 6.

FLAPJACKS AND HOT BLACK-BERRY JAM

Most of us have pancake mix in our cabinets or on the pantry shelves. If you ever have a craving for pancakes, and are out of mix, try Mama's flapjacks. She would make these when blackberries were ripe and serve them with hot blackberry jam. They are also good with sorghum molasses, or other syrups.

1½ cups self-rising flour
2 tbsp. sugar
1 egg, well beaten
1¼ cups milk
3 tbsp. melted butter

Mix flour and sugar together. Set aside. Mix beaten egg and milk together. Stir into flour, beating until smooth. Stir in melted butter. Grease hot skillet or grill. Pour enough batter on grill to make pancake about the size of a saucer. Turn to brown on both sides. Serve buttered with hot blackberry jam, sorghum molasses, or other syrup. Makes 6 flapjacks.

HOT BLACKBERRY JAM

Blackberries
Water to cover
Sugar

Wash blackberries. Put in saucepan with enough water to just cover berries. Let come to a boil. Simmer about 15 minutes. Put colander in large pan. Pour berries in colander, mashing to strain out all the juice. Some of the pulp and seeds will also come through. Discard what is left in colander.

Measure juice into a large pan. Add 1 cup sugar to every 1 cup of berry juice. Do not fill pan over ½ full or it will boil over. Mix sugar and juice. Put on medium heat. Bring to a boil. Boil briskly 30 minutes, stirring often the last 10 minutes. Remove from heat. Serve hot over buttered flapjacks or biscuits. Any leftovers can be put into jars and sealed. Will keep indefinitely.

MARGE'S STUFFED CABBAGE LEAVES

6 large outer leaves of cabbage
1 lb. ground beef
¼ tsp. black pepper
½ tsp. salt
½ tsp. chili powder
2 tsp. dried onion flakes
¼ tsp. garlic salt
⅛ tsp. oregano
⅓ cup uncooked rice
⅓ cup cracker crumbs
1 can (8 oz.) tomato sauce
1 cup water

Put cabbage leaves in boiling water about 5 minutes to soften. Mix ground beef and all other ingredients, except tomato sauce and water. Divide meat mixture evenly into middle of cabbage leaves. Wrap leaves around meat like wrapping blanket around baby. Place in large skillet or saucepan. Pour tomato sauce and water over all and let come to a boil. Turn heat down to simmer. Let simmer about 1½ hours. Serves 6.

HAMBURGER STEAK

1 lb. ground beef
1 tbsp. soy sauce
1 tbsp. steak sauce
¼ tsp. salt
¼ tsp. black pepper
2 onions, sliced

Mix ground beef, soy sauce, steak sauce, and salt. Make into 2 oval-shaped patties. Put in skillet. Sprinkle with half the black pepper. Cook over medium heat until brown, about 5 minutes. Turn and put sliced onions on top. Sprinkle with remaining black pepper. Cover and cook until onions are tender and steaks brown, about 5 minutes.

MEAT LOAF

1 lb. ground beef
¼ cup ketchup
¼ cup evaporated milk
¼ cup flour
1 egg, beaten
2 tsp. dried onion flakes
½ tsp. salt
¼ tsp. black pepper

Mix all ingredients together with hands. Shape into loaf. Put into greased loaf pan. Bake in 350-degree oven for 45 minutes. Remove from oven. Drizzle more ketchup on top. Let set 10 minutes before slicing. Serves 6.

POT ROAST

Meat tenderizer
1 chuck or shoulder roast (3 to
   4 lb.)
2 tbsp. flour
1 tbsp. butter or margarine
2 cups water
1 cup water
1 tbsp. flour
6 potatoes, peeled and quartered
6 carrots, scraped and cut into 2-
   inch pieces
1 tsp. salt
¼ tsp. black pepper

Use meat tenderizer on meat as directed on tenderizer bottle. Sprinkle 2 tbsp. flour on meat, patting to make it stick. Melt butter in Dutch oven. Add roast. Put in 450-degree oven, uncovered. Cook 15 minutes. Remove from oven and turn roast to brown on other side. Cook 15 minutes more.

Add 2 cups water, cover pot, and turn oven down to 350 degrees. Cook 1 hour, checking once to see if more water is needed. After 1 hour, remove from oven. Stir together 1 cup water and 1 tbsp. flour until smooth. Remove roast from pan and stir flour mixture into pan.

Return roast to gravy and add potatoes, carrots, salt, and pepper. Put lid back on. Cook in 350-degree oven 45 minutes longer. Remove from oven. Put roast on serving platter, arranging carrots and potatoes as desired. Pour gravy over all. Serves 8.

SKILLET HASH

2 tbsp. margarine
2 cups chopped leftover pot roast,
   or however much you have
2 cups peeled and chopped
   potatoes
1 cup chopped onions
½ tsp. salt
¼ tsp. black pepper
½ cup gravy from pot roast, or
   water if no gravy is left

Melt margarine in skillet. Add roast, potatoes, and onions. Sprinkle with salt and pepper. Cook over medium heat, turning to brown on both sides. Add gravy or water. Put on lid. Simmer about 10 minutes, stirring often. Taste to see if more salt is needed before serving. Serves 8.

COUNTRY HAM AND RED-EYE GRAVY

Country ham
⅔ cup water

In heavy skillet, fry country ham until brown on both sides. Remove from skillet. Pour grease drippings into heavy bowl. Add water to hot skillet. Let come to a boil, scraping brown bits from bottom of skillet. Pour into grease in bowl. Serve over eggs and biscuits with the ham.

SHEPHERD'S PIE

1 lb. ground beef
½ cup chopped onion
1 tbsp. flour
¼ tsp. salt
⅛ tsp. black pepper
½ cup beef broth
2 cups creamed potatoes
½ cup grated cheddar cheese

Place beef and onion in skillet. Sprinkle with flour, salt, and pepper. Brown beef and onion, stirring to break apart as it cooks. Drain. Put back in skillet. Add beef broth. Simmer about 10 to 15 minutes. Put into greased pie plate or casserole. Spread creamed potatoes on top. Bake in 375-degree oven for 20 minutes. Remove from oven. Sprinkle with cheese. Return to oven until cheese melts. Serves 6.

PORK CHOPS AND RICE

6 pork chops
2½ cups water
1 envelope onion soup mix
1 can cream of mushroom soup
1 cup rice, uncooked

Brown chops in skillet. Remove chops. Pour off grease. Add water to skillet, stirring and scraping brown bits from bottom of skillet. Put onion soup mix, mushroom soup, and rice in 13-by-9-inch baking pan. Pour the water over rice-soup mixture. Stir to combine. Place chops on top. Cover pan with foil. Bake in 350-degree oven for 1 hour. Serves 6.

CHOPPED BEEF ON TOAST

Marge, my sister-in-law, gave me this recipe. She once worked in a restaurant where this was actually listed on the menu by an obscene name. Mama would simply not tolerate ugly talk in her presence, and she never refrained from shaming a person for talking ugly. She once received an obscene phone call. After the caller had made his proposition, she said, "Oh, son, aren't you ashamed of yourself?! What would your mother say if she could hear you talking ugly like that? Who is your mother anyhow?" He hung up on her.

For Mama's sake, I'll call this chopped beef on toast.

3 tbsp. butter or margarine
3 tbsp. flour
2 cups milk
8 oz. thin-sliced cooked beef,
   chopped
Toast

The beef can be bought in the deli or lunch meat section. In heavy skillet, over medium heat, melt butter. Add flour, stirring to mix, and cook about 2 minutes. Add milk and stir until it begins to thicken, about 5 minutes. Turn heat on simmer. Add chopped beef. Continue to simmer about 10 minutes, stirring occasionally. Serve over toast. Serves 4 to 6.

PORK TENDERLOIN

When butchering a hog, Papa always cut the lean meat from the bone instead of making pork chops, leaving the backbone for boiling. I once purchased a slab of tenderloin in a grocery store, but the taste did not compare with the tenderloin I remember Mama cooking.

Pork tenderloin
1 tbsp. lard
½ cup water
Salt

Slice tenderloin in about ¼-inch pieces. Sprinkle with salt. Melt lard in heavy skillet. Brown meat on both sides, about 5 minutes per side. Remove to platter. Pour drippings into a heavy bowl. Place skillet back on stove. Pour in water, scraping up brown bits. Pour in bowl over drippings. This should make beautiful red-eye gravy.

BOILED BACKBONE

Backbone
2 tsp. salt
Water to cover
Black pepper

Place backbone in large kettle. Sprinkle with salt. Cover with water and bring to a boil. Cover pot and simmer 1½ hours, or until meat is fork tender. Remove to serving dish. Sprinkle generously with black pepper. Use broth to make dressing or soup. To make dressing, simply substitute backbone broth for chicken broth in the dressing from the Chicken and Dressing with Giblet Gravy recipe.

For soup, add chopped potatoes, onions, carrots, a handful of uncooked macaroni, maybe a chopped tomato or two, a sprinkling of basil, and salt and pepper. Let cook 30 minutes. Thicken with paste of 1 tablespoon flour and 1 cup water. Mmm-mmm good!

BRAINS AND EGGS

½ lb. hog brains
Boiling water to cover
1 tbsp. vinegar
6 eggs
2 tbsp. milk
Salt and pepper, to taste
2 tbsp. butter or margarine

Put brains in saucepan. Cover with boiling water. Add vinegar and simmer about 10 minutes. Drain and rinse, removing all membrane you possibly can while carefully pulling brains apart. Beat eggs with milk, salt, and pepper. Stir in the brains. Melt butter in skillet. Add brains and eggs. Stir constantly over medium heat until thickened. Serves 6.

RIBS AND SAUERKRAUT

4 lb. lean pork ribs
½ tsp. salt
¼ tsp. pepper
1 can (1 lb.) chopped sauerkraut
1 cup peeled and diced apple

Place ribs in baking pan. Sprinkle with salt and pepper. Cover with foil and bake in 350-degree oven for 1 hour. Remove foil and ribs and drain off fat. Mix kraut and apples together. Pour into bottom of baking pan. Place ribs on top. Put back in oven uncovered for 45 minutes, or until ribs are brown and tender. Serves 6.

FRIED HOG JOWL

It was New Year's Day and the sun was shining, a perfect day to do the laundry that had accumulated over the holidays. Having just finished hanging the third batch of washed clothes on the line, I heard the phone ringing. It was Mama.

She said, "I hope you weren't hanging out clothes." I said, "Why, Mama?" Mama said, "Don't you remember? It's bad luck to hang clothes on the line on New Year's Day. Do you have any hog jowl and black-eyed peas?" "Yes, Mama, I bought some Saturday. They had peas and hog jowl on special." "That's good," she said. "Cook them today and be sure everybody eats some for good luck." "Okay, Mama."

I really didn't lie to her; after all, she didn't come right out and ask me if I had clothes hanging on the line. It would have worried her terribly if she knew I had three lines hanging full of wet laundry. I decided to take a chance on the bad luck and just hoped Mama wouldn't come over until the clothes got dry.

I don't remember if the hanging laundry canceled out the good luck of the peas and hog jowl, or if the peas and hog jowl canceled out the bad luck of the hanging laundry. I do know that was the year our perfectly beautiful baby girl was born. That much good luck I remember.

Hog jowl
Salt if needed

Hog jowl can be bought in most grocery stores either cured or fresh. If cooking fresh hog jowl, sprinkle each side with salt. Cured needs no salt. Cut about 3 gashes in the skin of each slice. This prevents the meat from curling up as it cooks. Place in skillet over medium heat. Brown on both sides, 3 to 5 minutes per side.

FRIED MIDDLIN' MEAT

Boiling water
Sliced middling meat
Self-rising flour

Pour boiling water over sliced middling meat, sometimes called salt meat, streak-of-lean, or fatback. Stir around and let set 5 or 10 minutes. Pour off and rinse with hot water from faucet. Dredge meat in flour. Add 1 tablespoon grease to heavy skillet. Fry on medium heat till brown, 3 to 5 minutes per side.

DEER STEAKS AND GRAVY

Deer steaks
Meat tenderizer
Black pepper
Self-rising flour
Oil

Sprinkle steaks with meat tenderizer. Pound with meat mallet. Sprinkle heavily with black pepper. Dredge in flour. Fry in deep hot oil 5 to 8 minutes. To make gravy, drain all but 2 tablespoons oil from frying pan. Stir in 2 tablespoons flour. Cook until brown. Add 1 cup milk, stirring constantly until thickened. Add ¼ teaspoon black pepper and ½ teaspoon salt. Serve with steaks.

MOUNTAIN OYSTERS

Mountain oysters are the testicles cut from a male pig to keep the meat from being strong when he is grown. Although I have seen these once—and only once—in a grocery store, you will probably have to consult with a hog farmer as to when he will have a batch of hogs ready to cut and ask him to save them for you. They are usually thrown away, but Mama always cooked them and they are delicious. They are called mountain oysters because they are—as are oysters—a delicacy, meaning something choice or scarce.

6 to 10 mountain oysters
2 tbsp. salt
½ cup vinegar
2 qt. water
Salt and pepper
2 cups self-rising flour
½ cup cooking oil
2 tbsp. flour
1 cup water
1 cup milk

Beat meat with a meat mallet. Place in large pot. Add 2 tbsp. salt and vinegar. Pour 2 qt. water over meat, stirring around to dissolve salt. Put in refrigerator for 24 hours. Drain and wash meat. Sprinkle with salt and pepper. Dredge in 2 cups flour.

Fry in Dutch oven in hot oil until brown on both sides. Remove meat from oil. Drain in colander. Pour out all but 2 tbsp. of oil. Add 2 tbsp. flour to oil in pan. Stir and cook until brown. Add 1 cup water and the milk, stirring as you do. Turn heat to simmer. Place meat back into gravy. Cover with tight-fitting lid. Simmer 15 to 20 minutes. Serve with creamed potatoes or rice and biscuits. Serves 6.

FRIED TENNESSEE RIVER CATFISH

White Tennessee River catfish are said to be the best eating catfish in the world.

4 lb. catfish
1 tbsp. salt
Water to cover
Cooking oil
2 cups self-rising cornmeal

Cut fish into ½-inch steaks. Place in large container. Sprinkle with salt. Cover with water, stirring to dissolve salt. Pour oil into Dutch oven or skillet to depth of about 2 inches. Turn on high heat. Put cornmeal in plastic bag. Drop in fish, shaking to coat fish. Place fish in hot oil. Fry until brown on both sides, about 15 minutes per side. Drain in colander. Serve hot. Serves 8.

SALMON PATTIES

We'd had our regular Saturday in town. Mama, Johnnie, and I were waiting in the car parked near the new Piggly Wiggly store, while Papa rounded up the older kids for the trip home. Mama saw this as a chance to go looking in the store without a bunch of youngins tagging along. She told Johnnie and me to stay in the car and when Papa returned to say she wouldn't be long.

That store sure was a curiosity to Mama, she being used to trading at the neighborhood store where you asked for what you wanted and the storekeep got it off the shelf for you. You never "bothered" anything till it was bought and paid for. Piggly Wiggly wasn't doing much business, what with people not understanding how it worked with its rolling steel baskets and help-yourself ways. Most folks were like Mama—just lookers.

The man running the store was from some big city and didn't understand the ways of small-town country folk. Mama had herself a grand time going up one aisle and down another, picking up things she'd never seen before, reading the label, and putting it back on the shelf. She picked up a can of salmon thinking how nice it'd be to have fish that didn't have to be cleaned. However, after noting the price of the can and figuring she would need several to have enough for her brood, she placed it back on the shelf. Mama walked past the cashier saying "hidy doo" with a kind of guilt feeling because she had enjoyed herself so much and wasn't buying anything. As she walked out, that city fella, in his double-breasted suit, who had been standing by the door, took her by the arm and said, "All right, lady, let's go back in the store and see what you got in your hand bag."

Poor Mama didn't know what was going on. He guided her back into the store and insisted she empty the contents of her purse on the counter right in front of everyone. He was so sure Mama had stolen something and when he found nothing in the purse he said, "What did you do with that can of salmon?! I saw you take it off the shelf."

Mama explained that she just read the label and put it back and that she had never "stole" anything in her life. After thoroughly embarrassing and humiliating her he let her go without even an apology. When Mama got back to the car she was white as a sheet and trembling all over. Papa said, "What's wrong with you, Eva? Are you sick?" Mama, trying not to cry, replied, "I'll tell when we get home. I just want to go home."

When we arrived home Papa steered Mama into the parlor alone. We were all waiting outside the door to find out what was wrong with Mama. Papa burst out the parlor door with fire in his eyes! He roared, "Youngins, your Mama's in there crying her eyes out! That city slicker of a manager down to the Piggly Wiggly store accused her of stealing! I got to go set that man straight!" Top said, "I'll go, Papa! Me and Austin, we'll go! Mama needs you to stay here with her. I'll make that 'fereigner' understand our Mama ain't no thief. Don't you worry 'bout that!"

Top was not a big man, but he was young and had bulging muscles from working in the fields, and was strong as an ox! When Top and

Austin got to the store the man in the double-breasted suit was nowhere to be seen. Top shouted, "I come to see the man who runs this place!" The cashier explained, "He's in his office in back of the store."

The sign on the door said, "Oliver Dunwoody, Store Manager." Top didn't bother opening the door the usual way, just kicked it open. There sat Mr. Dunwoody behind a big desk in a swivel chair. He looked up kind of startledlike, probably thinking he was about to be robbed, and said, "Who are you?!"

Top yelled, "I'm Joe Robert Lock, son of the woman you accused of stealing today, and I'm gonna whup you good!" Top spun him around in that swivel chair and lifted him up, pushing him up against the wall. He wanted to smash his nose in so bad, but he could see the man was greying at the temples, and Top had been taught not to hit an older man, one who could not properly defend himself.

Mr. Dunwoody looked very frightened and was repeating over and over, "I'm sorry, it was just a mistake."

Top said, "You mighty right it wuz a mistake, a bad mistake. I'm not gonna hit you. I've been told not to hit my elders. You just better be glad Papa didn't come after ya. He could've hit you and he would've." After Mr. Dunwoody assured Top he would apologize to Mama, Top let him go.

We all tried to get Mama to go back in the store and get the apology she had coming, but she said, "We'll just forget it. He's new in town and just don't know how honest the folk around here are." However, Top was so mad and hurt over the matter he just couldn't let it go. He went to Mr. Charlie, an educated big landowner and friend of the family, to see what could be done.

Mr. Charlie said, "You're right, son. He must make a formal apology to your mother. I'll go with you to see him." Mr. Charlie suggested Mr. Dunwoody make a statement in the local paper and he readily agreed. It read: "Public apology—I, Oliver Dunwoody, Manager of Piggly Wiggly Grocery, apologize for any embarrassment I have caused Mrs. Eva Lock. Her son thoroughly convinced me that Mrs. Lock, is not, nor could she ever be, a thief. Please forgive me, Mrs. Lock." Soon afterward Mr. Dunwoody left the store. This satisfied Top to some degree.

A local man was hired as manager, people began to accept the store, and business prospered. Soon after Mama's ordeal, Papa brought a sack in from Rucker's Grocery and placed it on the table. He said, "Look what I brung ya, Eva." Mama reached in the sack and pulled out a can of salmon. There were four cans in the sack—enough for everybody! Papa explained, "I thought you deserved some of that fish you wuz accused of stealin'." Papa never said, but I got me an idy he asked Mr. Rucker to order up some salmon just for Mama.

This is Mama's recipe for Salmon Patties.

> **1 can (15 ½ oz.) salmon,**
> **   undrained**
> **1 egg, beaten**
> **¼ cup flour**
> **½ cup cracker crumbs**
> **3 tbsp. cooking oil or shortening**

Remove bone and skin from salmon. Add beaten egg, flour, and cracker crumbs. Mix with hands. Shape into patties. Place oil in skillet. Fry patties in hot oil, turning to brown on both sides, 5 to 8 minutes per side. Makes 8 to 10 patties.

SMOTHERED RABBIT

With Papa's help, Top made four rabbit gums (traps) and set them in the orchard. Every morning before going to school he'd check them, sometimes finding a rabbit in each gum. After they were skinned and cut up, Mama would put them to soak in salt water all day and have smothered rabbit for supper.

When word got out of the abundant supply of rabbits Top was catching, he began to get requests from people to buy his rabbits. Top was in the rabbit business. At twenty-five cents each he was earning spending money, something most boys his age didn't have.

When he brought two rabbits to school one day, and the teacher paid him a shiny half-dollar for them, it made quite an impression on the Weeks boys. They began to ask Top questions as to where his rabbit gums were located. Being a naïve young boy, he told them of his good luck in the orchard.

The next morning, when Top went to run his gums, they were nowhere to be seen. He knew right away who had taken them. With Chock and Austin backing him, he intended to go over to the Weeks' house and demand his rabbit gums back. But Papa said, "Now listen, son. You can't do that. The Weeks are our neighbors and you can't go accusing them of stealing. Mr. Weeks always holds up for his boys and it would just cause trouble. Think for a minute. Where would you set rabbit gums if you were the Weeks boys?"

"That's easy," Top said. "In the sagebrush patch just this side of their house."

Papa said, "All right, let's get up in the morning by daylight and go see how many rabbits you caught in the sagebrush patch."

Sure enough, there in the sagebrush patch were Top's rabbit gums with rabbits in them. He just left them there the remainder of the winter, getting up and running them before the Weeks boys. He caught more rabbits in the sagebrush patch than he ever did in the orchard, and the Weeks boys never knew.

1 rabbit, cut up
2 tsp. salt
Water to cover
2 cups self-rising flour
½ cup shortening
2 cups milk

Wash rabbit thoroughly. Put into large container. Sprinkle with salt and cover with water. Let soak in refrigerator overnight if possible. Drain. Dredge in flour. Fry in hot shortening, turning to brown on both sides. Remove rabbit from shortening.

Pour out all but 2 tablespoons of shortening. Add 2 tablespoons flour to shortening in skillet, stirring until a light brown. Add the milk. Continue to stir until thickened. Add rabbit to gravy. Turn heat to simmer. Place lid on skillet. Cook 30 minutes, or till rabbit is tender, checking during cooking time to see if more milk needs to be added to gravy. Serves 6.

SQUIRREL STEW WITH POTATO DUMPLINGS

2 squirrels, cleaned and cut up
1 tbsp. salt
½ cup vinegar
Water to cover

Put squirrels in large container. Sprinkle with salt. Add vinegar and enough water to cover squirrels. Stir to mix. Cover and place in refrigerator at least 2 hours or overnight.

STEW
2 qt. water
½ cup onions
1 tsp. salt, or to taste
¼ tsp. black pepper
1 cup water
1½ tbsp. flour

Drain squirrels and rinse. Put in large stew pot and add 2 qt. water, onions, salt, and pepper. Let come to a boil. Turn heat to low. Cover pot and simmer 1 hour, or until squirrel is tender. Make thickener of 1 cup water and the flour, stirring until smooth. Add to stew. If too thick, add more water. Let come to a boil again. Drop in dumplings by teaspoonfuls. Turn heat down. Cover and simmer 15 minutes. Serves 8.

POTATO DUMPLINGS

2 cups mashed potatoes
2 tbsp. finely chopped onion
1 egg, beaten
½ cup flour
¼ tsp. salt
⅛ tsp. black pepper

Mix all dumpling ingredients together. Cook as directed above.

THICKENING GRAVY

2 tbsp. flour
2 tbsp. ham, bacon, or sausage
   drippings
1 cup milk
½ tsp. salt

Stir flour into drippings. Cook over medium heat till light brown (about 3 minutes). Pour in milk. Continue to stir till thickened (5 to 8 minutes). Add salt. Good for sopping, or over eggs, potatoes, or rice. Serves 4 to 6.

Vegetables

Looking down the road from our mailbox.

BAKED ACORN SQUASH

Acorn squash
Melted butter
Salt
Brown sugar or honey

The rind of acorn squash is hard, making it difficult to peel; therefore, it is easier to prepare if the rind is left on while cooking.

Cut squash in half. Bake cut-side down in shallow baking pan in 350-degree oven for 35 minutes. Turn cut-side up. Brush with melted butter and sprinkle with salt. Sprinkle with brown sugar or drizzle with honey. Bake about 20 minutes more, until pulp is tender.

SOUR CREAM YELLOW SQUASH

2 lb. yellow squash, cooked and
drained
¼ cup butter or margarine
½ cup sour cream
¼ cup chopped green onion
½ tsp. salt
⅛ tsp. white pepper
1 cup fresh bread crumbs
¼ cup parmesan cheese
3 tbsp. melted butter

Mix squash and next 5 ingredients together. Place in 2-quart casserole. Mix bread crumbs, cheese, and melted butter together. Sprinkle on top of squash. Bake in 350-degree oven for 25 minutes. Serves 6 to 8.

STIR FRIED SQUASH

In our small town it is never necessary to lock your car, except when squash is in season. Just a few squash vines will produce more than even a large family can consume. Everyone who raises squash is more than willing to share with anyone who will accept. If you leave your car unlocked and parked on the square you're likely to find a big sack of squash, or maybe even two, left by a well-meaning neighbor. So I've developed many ways to prepare squash, for I would invariably forget to lock my car and find myself overrun with the abundantly producing vegetable.

2 tbsp. butter or margarine
About 4 cups chopped squash,
   yellow or zucchini
1 cup chopped onion
½ tsp. salt, or to taste
2 cups chopped fresh tomatoes
1 can (4 oz.) green chilies
2 cups cooked rice
½ cup grated parmesan cheese

In skillet, melt butter and add squash, onion, salt, and tomatoes. Cook about 15 minutes, stirring occasionally. Add chilies and cook 5 minutes more. Spoon over rice. Sprinkle with cheese. Serves 6.

ASPARAGUS WITH CHEESE SAUCE

2 tbsp. butter or margarine
2 tbsp. self-rising flour
2 cups milk
¼ tsp. salt
⅛ tsp. black pepper
1 cup shredded cheddar cheese
2 lb. fresh asparagus, cooked

In heavy saucepan, melt butter. Add flour. Cook until bubbly, about 2 minutes. Add milk, salt, and pepper. Cook, stirring constantly until thickened, 5 to 8 minutes. Add cheese. Remove from heat. Stir until cheese melts. Pour over asparagus. Serves 6 to 8.

GREEN BEANS, POTATOES, AND ONIONS

5 or 6 cups fresh green beans
Water to cover
3 medium potatoes
1 large onion
1 tsp. salt
3 tbsp. fried meat grease

Place beans in large pot. Cover with water. Bring to boil. Turn heat down and boil slowly for 30 minutes. Peel potatoes. Cut in quarters, then half-quarters. Lay on top of beans. Peel and quarter onion. Lay on top of potatoes and beans. Sprinkle with salt and add grease. May need to add water, but do not add too much. The beans should be almost dry when potatoes and onions are done. Cook an additional 15 to 20 minutes, until potatoes and onions are tender. Serves 6.

HOPPING JOHN

**1 cup salt pork, cut into small
  chunks
½ cup chopped onion
½ cup chopped green pepper
2 cans (15 oz.) black-eyed peas
¾ cup tomato juice
⅓ cup uncooked rice**

Cook salt pork in large skillet until brown. Add onion and green pepper. Sauté until tender. Add peas, tomato juice, and rice. Bring to a boil. Cover and reduce heat to simmer for 20 minutes. Serves 6.

BLACK-EYED PEAS

Although Mama put up dozens of cans of fresh peas, there were always many peas left in the patch that dried on the vines. We gathered the dried ones in a cotton sack and beat them with a stick, making the dried pods pop open and thus eliminating much of the shelling.

To prepare fresh peas, simply wash and put in large pot. Cover with water and boil about 20 minutes. Add fried meat grease, salt to taste, and boil another 15 minutes, being sure to have plenty of water in them so as to be soupy for sopping with corn bread.

Dried peas are cooked in the same fashion, although they will need to cook longer and have more water added from time to time.

BEANS AND HAM HOCKS

Many a Southern family has been raised on dried beans and corn bread. Early in the morning Mama often filled her big iron pot with Great Northern or pinto beans and set them on the stove to cook until dinnertime. With fried middlin' meat and corn bread, this made some mighty good eating.

There were usually some beans left, to which Mama added potatoes, onions, a can of her home-canned tomatoes, and corn. The pot was once again full and put back on the stove to simmer the rest of the day, making a delicious soup for supper.

> **2 cups Great Northern or pinto**
> **beans**
> **4 cups water**
> **2 ham hocks**
> **Salt to taste**

Wash beans. Put in large pot. Add water. Wash ham hocks. Put on top of beans. Let come to a boil. Turn heat to low. Put lid on pot. Cook 2 hours, checking often to see if more water is needed. Remove ham. Pull meat from bones. Discard bones and skin. If you have a hound dog, give it to him. Chop meat and add back to beans. Add salt to taste. Good with corn bread and Wilted Lettuce Salad (see index for recipes). Serves 8.

ENGLISH PEAS AND POTATOES

1 can (16 oz.) green English peas
2 medium potatoes
2 tbsp. butter or margarine
½ tsp. salt

Place peas in saucepan. Peel potatoes. Cut in quarters, then half-quarters. Lay on top of peas. Add butter and salt. Cover pan and simmer 15 to 20 minutes until potatoes are tender. Serves 4 to 6.

PEAS AND OKRA

About 5 cups fresh purple hull or
**   black-eyed peas**
Water to cover
2 tbsp. fried meat grease
1 tsp. salt
8 to 10 small pods okra

Place peas in large saucepan. Add enough water to cover peas. Bring to boil. Turn heat down and boil slowly for 10 minutes. Add 1 tbsp. meat grease, ½ tsp. salt, and more water if needed to cover peas. Cook 10 minutes longer. Lay whole okra pods on top of peas. Sprinkle with remaining grease and salt.

Cover pot and cook 15 minutes more, until okra is tender. Lift okra out and put in separate bowl. The pea juice gives the okra a really good flavor. Taste peas and add more salt if needed. Corn on the cob is also delicious cooked on top of peas. Serves 6 to 8.

FRIED OKRA

This is a simple and delicious dish.

Okra pods
Self-rising cornmeal
Oil

Cut stems from okra pods. Cut into ½-inch slices. Dredge in corn-meal. Fry in deep hot oil until brown, about 5 minutes. Drain in colander.

FRIED CABBAGE

1 cabbage head
1 cup water
½ tsp. salt, or to taste
1 tbsp. fried meat grease or
shortening
3 tbsp. butter or margarine

Slice cabbage in about ¼-inch slices. Discard the core and tough bottom stems. Place cabbage in large Dutch oven. Add water and salt. Cover with tight-fitting lid and cook until cabbage is tender, about 15 minutes. Melt grease and butter in skillet. With slotted spoon, lift cabbage from pot into skillet. Cook, stirring, about 5 minutes. Taste to see if more salt is needed. Remove from heat and serve. Serves 6.

FRIED GREEN TOMATOES

4 to 6 medium green tomatoes
1 tbsp. salt
Water to cover
1 cup self-rising flour
1 cup self-rising cornmeal
Fat

Core and slice tomatoes about ¼ inch thick. Put in large bowl. Sprinkle with salt. Cover with water, stirring to mix in the salt. Mix flour and cornmeal together. Remove tomato slices from water a few at a time. Dredge in flour-cornmeal mixture. Fry in deep hot fat until brown on both sides, about 5 minutes per side. Serves 6.

FRIED TATERS
(Hash Browns)

4 cups chopped potatoes
4 tbsp. fried meat grease
1 tsp. salt

Peel and chop potatoes into small pieces. Put grease in skillet and heat till hot. Add potatoes and sprinkle with salt. Put tight lid on skillet and turn heat to low. After about 10 minutes, turn potatoes to brown on other side. Use slotted spoon to lift up into bowl. Serves 6.

POTATO PANCAKES

2 cups fresh or leftover salted
   mashed potatoes
1 egg, beaten
¼ cup chopped onion
½ cup self-rising flour
3 tbsp. cooking oil or shortening

Mix together potatoes, beaten egg, onion, and flour. With floured hands, make into patties. Fry in hot oil, turning to brown on both sides, about 5 minutes per side. Makes about 10 pancakes.

STEWED "ARSH PATATERS"

4 medium Irish (red) potatoes
Water to cover
½ tsp. salt
1 tbsp. fried meat grease
1 tbsp. butter or margarine
¼ tsp. black pepper
1 tbsp. flour
1 cup water
½ cup grated cheddar cheese

Peel and coarsely chop potatoes. Place in large saucepan. Add enough water to cover potatoes. Add salt and boil 15 minutes. Add grease, butter, and pepper. Continue to simmer. Make a paste of the flour and 1 cup water, mixing with fork until smooth. Pour into potatoes. Add more water if too thick. Taste and add more salt if needed. Cook about 5 or 10 minutes more. Serve as is or mash slightly with fork and serve in soup bowls. Sprinkle top with grated cheese. Serves 4.

EASY GLAZED SWEET POTATOES

**2 cans (1 lb. 7 oz. each) sweet
   potatoes, drained
½ cup butter, melted
½ cup pineapple preserves or
   orange marmalade
½ cup sliced almonds, toasted**

Place potatoes in 10-by-6-inch baking dish. Pour melted butter over potatoes. Top with preserves or marmalade. Bake in 350-degree oven for 30 minutes, basting occasionally. Sprinkle with toasted almonds. Serves 6 to 8.

ROST NERS
(Roasted Ears)

I thought up till I was grown that "Rost Ners" was the proper name for roasted ears of corn. Mama never had aluminum foil to wrap corn in, so she just baked them in their shucks.

**6 or more ears of corn
Water
Butter to taste
Salt to taste**

Pull shucks down on corn, but do not remove or break them off. Remove silks. Pull shucks back up in place. Tie with a string. Soak corn in water about 30 minutes. Drain. Put in bread pan. Bake in 350-degree oven for about 45 minutes. Pull down shucks, being careful not to burn your hands. You may need to use a potholder. Spread with fresh-churned butter and sprinkle with salt. Serves 6.

CORN PUDDING

3 eggs
1 can (17 oz.) cream-style corn
1 can (4 oz.) chopped green
   chilies, drained
1 cup shredded sharp cheddar
   cheese
½ tsp. salt
1 pimiento, chopped

Beat eggs. Add other ingredients. Pour into greased 8-inch square baking pan. Bake in 325-degree oven for 45 minutes. Serves 8.

FRIED CORN

The secret to good fried corn is the corn selected and the way it is cut from the cob. Corn is right for making good cream-style fried corn when the silks are dark but not dry, and the kernels burst and juice runs out when punctured with your fingernail. Field corn is best for fried corn, but if you aren't raising your own, or don't have a farm friend who raises corn, it is difficult to find. Most supermarkets sell only sweet corn.

6 large ears fresh field corn
1 tbsp. fried meat grease
Water
4 tbsp. butter or margarine
½ tsp. salt, or to taste

Shuck and silk corn. In large pan or bowl place ear of corn on end. With sharp knife cut all the way down the ear, just barely slicing off the top of the kernel. After cutting all the way around the ear, go back and scrape the cob. The juice and insides of the kernel is what makes the corn thick and creamy. Proceed with all ears. (Your glasses and all other objects around will be splattered with corn juice, but the results are worth it.)

Grease large skillet with fried meat grease. Pour in corn. Mix enough water with corn to make it soupy. Add butter and salt, tasting to see if more salt is needed. It's okay to taste raw corn! Cook on medium heat, stirring often until thickened, about 15 or 20 minutes. Serves 6 to 8.

VEGETABLE CASSEROLE

This dish is good using squash, broccoli, or asparagus.

4 cups cooked vegetables (squash, broccoli, or asparagus)
1 can (10¾ oz.) cream of mushroom soup
1 cup cooked rice
1 cup bread crumbs
1 tbsp. dried onion flakes
1½ cups grated cheddar cheese
½ tsp. salt
½ cup cracker crumbs, crushed
2 tbsp. margarine, melted

Drain cooked vegetables. Add soup, rice, bread crumbs, onion flakes, 1 cup of the cheese, and salt. Mix together. Put in greased casserole dish. Mix cracker crumbs with margarine. Sprinkle on top. Sprinkle remaining ½ cup cheddar cheese on top of cracker crumbs. Bake uncovered in 400-degree oven for 20 minutes. Serves 6 to 8.

TURNIP GREENS
(A Tennessee Staple)

Turnip greens
2 cups water
½ lb. salt pork
Salt to taste

Put as many fresh washed turnip greens in a large pot as you can and still get a lid on. Add water and salt pork cut into small chunks. Put on medium heat. Boil about 10 minutes. Stir down and add more water if needed. Boil with lid on another 20 minutes. Salt to taste. Serve with corn bread and a big slice of onion. Corn bread is good sopped in the pot liquor.

TURNIPS

Turnips are very good to eat raw. They are also very good boiled and served with corn bread. For a real treat, crumble or sop your corn bread in the juice.

5 or 6 medium turnips
Water to cover
½ tsp. salt, or to taste
2 tbsp. butter or margarine

Peel and quarter turnips. Place in saucepan. Cover with water. Add salt. Boil over medium heat about 15 minutes, or until tender. Add butter and more salt if needed. Cook 3 to 5 minutes longer. Enjoy! Serves 6.

COLLARD GREENS

2 lb. collards
½ lb. salt pork, chopped
2 qt. water
½ tsp. salt, or to taste

Cut off tough stems of collards. Place pork, water, and collards in large kettle. Bring to a boil. Turn heat down and boil gently with lid on kettle for 1 hour. Add salt. Taste to see if more salt is needed. Boil 15 to 20 minutes longer, or until greens are tender and liquid has boiled down low. Serves 6.

EGGPLANT CASSEROLE

2 medium eggplants, peeled and
 sliced
Water to cover
1 cup stewed canned tomatoes,
 chopped
½ cup bread crumbs
½ tsp. salt
¼ tsp. pepper
¼ tsp. oregano leaves
1 can (8 oz.) tomato sauce
1½ cups grated cheddar cheese
½ cup grated parmesan cheese

Place eggplants in saucepan. Cover with water and bring to a boil. Simmer 10 minutes. Drain. In 2-quart casserole dish, layer half of all ingredients in order given. Repeat layers. Bake uncovered in 350-degree oven for 20 minutes, until hot through. Serves 8.

PERRY COUNTY POKE SALLET

Mama could always count on Izzy to come on washday and help her with the wash. When she didn't arrive by daybreak, Mama said, "George, go see what's keepin' Izzy."

When Papa got there, Izzy said, "Mr. Joge, I wuz a-fixin' to come to yawl's place when ever'thang tarned jest green as pisen 'n I fell clean out right der on de flow."

Papa said, "Ah, Izzy, ain't nothin' wrong with you. You just been eatin' too much poke sallet."

Poke is a wild green that comes up every spring in the fencerows and along the roadsides of Tennessee. The taste is like spinach and is much sought after by true Tennesseans. It will have too strong a taste if it is not boiled, the water drained off, and fresh water added to cook. It may be prepared by simply boiling until tender and adding fried meat grease and salt. However, after moving to Perry County, I learned the following method of preparing the greens.

**1 grocery bag half-filled with
   young poke
3 cups water
½ cup chopped green onions
3 tbsp. fried meat grease
½ tsp. salt, or to taste
1 egg, beaten**

Wash poke thoroughly. Put in kettle with water. Bring to a boil. Stir down and let boil about 5 minutes. Drain and rinse. Return to pot. Add green onions and 1 cup fresh water. Boil again with lid on for 15 minutes. Drain. Put meat grease in iron skillet. Add poke and salt. Stir fry about 5 minutes. Add beaten egg and scramble until egg is done. Serve with corn bread, onion, and hot pepper sauce. Serves 6.

Cakes and Pies

Cousin Aldia Lock, 1922.

Cousin Bernice Robinson, 1925.

APPLE STACK CAKE

Mama dried her apples and peaches on the tin roof of the chicken house.

½ cup shortening
1¼ cups sugar
⅔ cup buttermilk
½ tsp. baking soda
1 tsp. ground ginger
4 cups self-rising flour

Cream together shortening and sugar. Add buttermilk. Add baking soda and ginger to flour. Add flour to creamed mixture a cup at a time until dough is stiff. Divide dough into 5 equal portions. Pat each portion into 5 greased 9-inch cake pans. Bake in 400-degree oven for 8 to 10 minutes, or until brown. Carefully remove layers to cooling rack. Stack cake layers, spreading filling between each layer.

FILLING

4 cups dried apples
2⅔ cups water
⅔ cup sugar
⅓ cup butter

Combine apples and water in heavy saucepan. Bring to a boil. Reduce heat. Add sugar and simmer 30 minutes, stirring often to prevent sticking. Remove from heat. Stir in butter. Put between layers of stack cake.

FRESH FRUIT CAKE

This is sometimes called Punch Bowl Cake and made in a punch bowl; however, I find it better to use a four-inch deep, thirteen-by-nine-inch plastic container, which can be purchased at any discount store.

1 box white or yellow cake mix
2 qt. fresh strawberries, sliced and
** sweetened**
3 containers (8 oz. each) whipped
** topping**
1 box (5½ oz.) vanilla instant
** pudding, prepared as directed**
2 cans (8 oz. each) crushed
** pineapple, drained**
2 bananas, sliced
1 can coconut flakes
1 cup chopped pecans
Whole strawberries for garnish

Prepare cake according to directions, using a 13-by-9-inch pan. Assemble in layers as follows.

First layer: Crumble ⅓ cake in bottom of plastic container. Layer ⅓ strawberries over crumbs. Spread 1 container whipped topping over strawberries.

Second layer: Crumble ⅓ cake over whipped topping. Layer ⅓ strawberries over crumbs. Cover with 1 container whipped topping. Spread all of instant pudding over topping. Layer all of pineapple over pudding and bananas over pineapple.

Third layer: Crumble ⅓ cake. Spread with remaining strawberries and remaining container of whipped topping. Sprinkle with coconut and nuts. Garnish with whole strawberries. Serves 20 or more, depending on size of serving.

LIGHT FRUITCAKE

1 lb. candied cherries
1 lb. candied pineapple
1 box (15 oz.) golden raisins
2 cups pecans, coarsely chopped
1 cup walnuts, coarsely chopped
1 cup shortening
1 cup sugar
1 tsp. vanilla
4 tbsp. orange juice
1 tbsp. grated orange rind
5 eggs
3 cups all-purpose flour
1 tbsp. baking powder
1 tsp. salt

Place fruit and nuts in large bowl. Mix well and set aside. Cream together shortening and sugar. Add vanilla, orange juice, and rind. Add eggs one at a time, beating well after each addition. Sift together flour, baking powder, and salt.

Mix half of flour into egg batter. Mix remaining half with fruit-nut mixture. Pour egg batter over fruit mixture, mixing with hands or large spoon to distribute nuts and fruit well throughout batter. Grease and flour 10-inch tube pan. Pour in batter.

Place pan of hot water on bottom rack of oven below cake. Bake cake in 300-degree oven for 2½ hours, or until wooden pick inserted in center comes out clean. Cool in pan 30 minutes. Run knife around sides of pan. Invert on wire rack to cool.

PRUNE CAKE

3 eggs, beaten
1 cup vegetable oil
1½ cups sugar
2 cups self-rising flour
1 tsp. allspice
1 tsp. cinnamon
1 tsp. nutmeg
1 cup milk
1 tsp. vanilla
1 cup cooked mashed prunes
1 cup chopped black walnuts or
  pecans

Combine eggs, oil, and sugar and mix well. Combine flour, allspice, cinnamon, and nutmeg. Add to oil mixture alternately with milk, beating well after each addition. Stir in vanilla, prunes, and nuts. Bake in greased and floured 13-by-9-inch pan at 350 degrees for 30 minutes, or until pick inserted in center comes out clean.

ICING

1 cup firmly packed brown sugar
½ tsp. baking soda
¼ cup butter or margarine
1 tbsp. corn syrup
½ cup buttermilk
½ tsp. vanilla

Combine all ingredients except vanilla in saucepan. Cook about 5 minutes, stirring constantly. Remove from heat. Add vanilla and beat well. Icing will have consistency of glaze. Pour on cake.

STRAWBERRY CAKE

1 box white cake mix
1 box (3 oz.) strawberry gelatin
½ cup water
½ cup cooking oil
4 eggs
½ cup frozen strawberries, thawed

Put cake mix, gelatin, water, and oil in mixing bowl. Mix until smooth. Beat in eggs one at a time. Add strawberries. Mix well. Bake in 2 greased and floured 9-inch cake pans at 350 degrees for 25 to 30 minutes. Cool before icing.

ICING

½ cup margarine
1 box (1 lb.) confectioners' sugar,
  sifted
½ cup frozen strawberries, thawed

Cream margarine. Add sugar in small amounts, beating after each addition. Add strawberries, as needed, to make beating easy. Spread between layers and on top of cool cake.

BROWNIE CAKE

4 eggs
2 cups sugar
1 cup melted butter or margarine
4 tbsp. cocoa powder, sifted
1 cup self-rising flour
1 cup chopped pecans

Beat eggs. Add sugar, melted butter, and cocoa. Stir in flour and pecans. Pour into greased and floured 13-by-9-inch baking pan. Bake in 325-degree oven for 20 minutes. Turn oven temperature to 350 degrees and bake 25 minutes more. Cool in pan. Spread with icing.

CHOCOLATE FUDGE ICING

2 cups sugar
⅓ cup cocoa powder
½ cup milk
¼ cup butter or margarine
½ tsp. vanilla

Mix sugar and cocoa. Add milk. Bring to a boil. Boil hard for 2 minutes. Remove from heat. Add butter and vanilla. Beat until smooth. Spread on cake.

DEVIL'S FOOD CAKE

1½ cups all-purpose flour
1½ cups sugar
1¼ tsp. baking soda
1 tsp. salt
⅓ cup cocoa
½ cup oil
1 cup milk
1 tsp. vanilla
3 eggs

Sift together dry ingredients. Add oil, milk, and vanilla. Beat 2 minutes, scraping bottom and sides of bowl. Add eggs. Beat 2 minutes more. Pour into two 8-inch greased and floured cake pans. Bake in 350-degree oven for 25 to 30 minutes. Frost with your favorite frosting.

AUNT IBBIE'S JAM CAKE

1 cup shortening
2 cups sugar
4 eggs
1 cup blackberry jam
1 tsp. baking soda
1 cup buttermilk
3 cups flour
1 tsp. cinnamon
1 tsp. allspice
½ tsp. salt

Cream shortening and sugar together until fluffy. Add eggs one at a time, beating well after each addition. Add jam, mixing well. Stir baking soda into buttermilk. Sift flour, spices, and salt together and add alternately with buttermilk to jam mixture, beginning and ending with flour.

Grease and flour three 9-inch cake pans. Pour batter into pans. Bake in 350-degree oven for 25 to 30 minutes, or until wooden pick inserted in center comes out clean. Let cool in pans about 5 minutes. Turn out on racks to cool.

FILLING

1 small can crushed pineapple
1½ cups sugar
1 tbsp. flour
⅓ cup water
¼ cup butter
1 cup golden raisins
1 cup chopped nuts
1 cup coconut flakes

Mix together pineapple, sugar, flour, and water. Cook in heavy saucepan over medium heat until thickened, about 10 minutes. Remove from heat. Add butter, raisins, nuts, and coconut. Spread between layers of cake.

CARAMEL ICING
4½ cups sugar, divided
⅛ tsp. salt
1½ cups milk
¾ cup butter or margarine
½ tsp. vanilla

Mix together 3 cups sugar, the salt, and the milk in heavy saucepan. Put over low heat, stirring frequently. Meanwhile place remaining 1½ cups sugar in iron skillet. Cook over medium heat until sugar dissolves and becomes brown and syrupy. Gradually pour into hot sugar-milk mixture in saucepan. Cook over medium heat, stirring often until mixture reaches soft ball stage. Remove from heat. Add butter and vanilla. Beat until thick enough to spread. Spread on top and sides of cake.

CHESS CAKE

1 box yellow cake mix
1 egg, beaten
½ cup margarine, melted
8 oz. cream cheese, softened
2 eggs, beaten
1 box (1 lb.) confectioners' sugar
1 cup chopped pecans

Mix together cake mix, 1 egg, and margarine. Press into a 13-by-9-inch baking pan. Beat cream cheese until smooth. Add 2 eggs and mix until smooth. Gradually beat in confectioners' sugar. Stir in nuts. Pour over cake mix in baking pan. Bake at 350 degrees for 30 minutes.

GENERAL ROBERT E. LEE CAKE

I feel that my cookbook, containing so many traditional Southern recipes, would not be complete without this cake. According to legend, Mary Custis was serving a piece of this cake to then Lt. Robert E. Lee when he proposed marriage. She accepted, thus joining together two of Virginia's most notable families, Robert being the son of Henry Lee, governor of Virginia, and Mary being the great-granddaughter of Martha Washington.

2 cups all-purpose flour
½ tsp. cream of tartar
1½ tsp. baking powder
8 eggs, separated
2 cups sugar
2 tsp. grated lemon rind
2 tbsp. lemon juice
¼ tsp. salt

Sift together first 3 ingredients. Set aside. Beat egg yolks until thick and lemon colored. Gradually add sugar. Stir in lemon rind and juice. Sprinkle salt over egg whites. Beat until soft peaks form. Fold into egg yolk mixture alternately with flour mixture.

Spoon batter into two greased and floured 9-inch cake pans. Bake in 325-degree oven for 25 minutes, or until wooden pick inserted in center comes out clean. Cool in pans for 10 minutes. Remove to wire racks to cool completely. Split layers horizontally. Spread lemon filling between layers. Chill 30 minutes to let set. Ice top and sides with lemon-orange icing. Sprinkle with coconut.

LEMON FILLING

4 egg yolks, beaten
1⅓ cups sugar
2 tsp. grated lemon rind
⅓ cup lemon juice
¼ cup butter

In top of double boiler, combine first 4 ingredients. Cook over boiling water, stirring constantly until sugar dissolves. Add butter and cook until thickened, about 20 minutes. Cool before spreading between cake layers.

LEMON-ORANGE ICING

⅓ cup butter or margarine,
   softened
4 cups sifted confectioners' sugar
3 tbsp. grated orange rind
2½ tbsp. orange juice
1½ tsp. grated lemon rind
1 tbsp. plus 1 tsp. lemon juice
½ cup finely grated coconut

Beat all ingredients except coconut together until smooth and creamy. Spread on top and sides of cake. Sprinkle with coconut.

GRANNY'S POUND CAKE

This cake is moist and delicious and so easy to make.

2 cups sugar
1 cup Crisco oil
4 eggs
1 cup milk
2 cups self-rising flour
1 tsp. vanilla

Mix together sugar and oil. Stir in eggs one at a time. Beat until smooth. Stir in milk alternately with flour, beginning and ending with flour. Add vanilla. Beat until smooth. Grease and flour tube pan. Pour in batter. Bake in 325-degree oven for 45 minutes, or until pick inserted in center comes out clean.

CHOCOLATE SUNDAE CAKE

When done, this is a cake on top with rich chocolate sauce on the bottom.

1 cup self-rising flour
¾ cup sugar
2 tbsp. cocoa
½ cup milk
⅓ cup butter or margarine, melted
1 tsp. vanilla
1 cup nuts, chopped
½ cup brown sugar
½ cup white sugar
¼ cup cocoa
1½ cups hottest tap water

In mixing bowl, stir together flour, ¾ cup sugar, and 2 tbsp. cocoa. Add milk, melted butter, and vanilla. Stir in nuts. Spread evenly in ungreased 9-by-9-inch pan. Mix brown sugar, white sugar, and ¼ cup cocoa. Sprinkle over batter. Pour hot water over all. Bake in 350-degree oven for 40 minutes. Let stand 15 minutes. Cut into squares and spoon into dessert dishes. Top with ice cream. Spoon sauce over ice cream.

FUNNEL CAKES

Funnel cakes are formed by letting the batter flow through a funnel into hot oil, swirling into a ring. To stop the flow of batter, close the funnel opening with your finger. These are delicious served with coffee for breakfast. A funnel with a ⅜-inch opening works best.

2½ cups self-rising flour
¼ cup sugar
1⅓ cups milk
2 eggs, well beaten
Vegetable oil
Sifted confectioners' sugar

Combine flour and sugar. Beat in milk and eggs until smooth. Heat ½ inch oil in skillet. Cover bottom opening of funnel with finger. Pour about ⅓ cup batter into funnel. Hold over skillet. Release batter into hot oil, moving funnel in a slow circular motion to form a circular cake. Fry until brown on one side (2 to 3 minutes). Turn to brown on other side (2 to 3 minutes). Drain on paper towels. Sprinkle with confectioners' sugar. Repeat with remaining batter. Makes 12 cakes.

SCRATCH CAKE

½ cup butter or margarine
1½ cups sugar
3 eggs
2¼ cups self-rising flour
1 cup milk
½ tsp. vanilla

Beat butter until creamy. Add sugar. Add eggs one at a time, beating after each addition until smooth. Add flour and milk alternately, beating until smooth, beginning and ending with flour. Add vanilla. Bake in 13-by-9 inch pan for 25 to 30 minutes, or until wooden pick inserted in center comes out clean. Ice as desired.

MISSISSIPPI MUD CAKE

½ cup butter, softened
1 cup sugar
3 eggs
¾ cup self-rising flour
¼ cup plus 1½ tbsp. cocoa
1 tsp. vanilla
1 cup chopped pecans
1 bag (10 oz.) miniature
  marshmallows

Cream butter and sugar together. Beat in eggs one at a time, beating well after each addition. Sift flour and cocoa together. Add to creamed mixture. Stir in vanilla and pecans. Spoon batter into a greased and flour-dusted 13-by-9-inch baking pan.

Bake in 325-degree oven for 15 to 18 minutes, or until pick inserted in center comes out clean. Remove from oven and cover top with marshmallows. Put back in oven about 2 minutes just to soften marshmallows, but not melt them. Cover immediately with icing.

ICING

¼ cup butter or margarine
⅓ cup cocoa
⅓ cup milk
1 box (1 lb.) confectioners' sugar
1 tsp. vanilla

Place butter, cocoa, and milk in heavy saucepan. Cook over medium heat until smooth and butter is melted. Beat in sugar and vanilla. Spread on warm cake.

CHOCOLATE CAKE

½ cup cocoa
½ cup boiling water
⅔ cup shortening
2 cups sugar
1 tsp. vanilla
2 eggs
2¼ cups all-purpose flour
1½ tsp. baking soda
½ tsp. salt
1⅓ cups buttermilk

Stir cocoa and boiling water together till smooth and set aside. Cream shortening, sugar, and vanilla. Add eggs. Beat well. Combine flour, baking soda, and salt. Add alternately with buttermilk to creamed mixture. Stir in cocoa and water. Pour into greased and floured 13-by-9-inch baking pan. Bake in 350-degree oven for 35 to 40 minutes, or until pick inserted in center comes out clean. Cool before icing.

ICING

½ cup butter or margarine
⅓ cup cocoa
3 cups confectioners' sugar, sifted
⅓ cup milk
1 tsp. vanilla

In saucepan over low heat, melt butter or margarine. Add cocoa, stirring till smooth. Remove from heat. Add sugar, milk, and vanilla. Pour on cake.

ELEGANT SPICE CAKE

2½ cups all-purpose flour
1 tsp. baking powder
1 tsp. baking soda
1 tsp. salt
1 tsp. cinnamon
½ tsp. ginger
¼ tsp. nutmeg
¼ tsp. cloves
½ cup light brown sugar
1 cup white sugar
½ cup oil
2 eggs
1 tsp. vanilla
¼ tsp. lemon extract
1¼ cups buttermilk

Sift first 8 ingredients together. Add sugars to oil. Beat until thoroughly mixed. Add eggs, vanilla, and lemon extract. Beat until mixed well. Add dry ingredients alternately with buttermilk, beginning and ending with flour mixture. Pour into two 9-inch greased and floured cake pans. Bake in 350-degree oven for 30 minutes, or until wooden pick inserted in center comes out clean. Ice with Caramel Icing.

PEACH BRANDY POUND CAKE

Mama never allowed liquor in the house; however, Papa did keep peach brandy in the cupboard for his cough. At Christmas time Mama would use a cup of the brandy for a delicious cake—that is, if there was any brandy to be had. Papa seldom got sick, but he sure coughed a lot.

1 cup butter or margarine,
  softened
3 cups sugar
6 eggs
3 cups all-purpose flour
¼ tsp. baking soda
½ tsp. salt
1 carton (8 oz.) sour cream
1 cup peach brandy
1 tsp. orange extract
½ tsp. lemon extract
1 tsp. vanilla extract
¼ tsp. almond extract

Cream butter. Gradually add sugar, beating until mixture is light and fluffy. Add eggs one at a time, beating well after each addition. Combine flour, baking soda, and salt. Combine sour cream, brandy, and flavorings. Add to creamed mixture alternately with flour mixture, beginning and ending with flour. Pour batter into greased and floured 10-inch tube pan. Bake at 325 degrees for 1 hour and 20 minutes. Cool in pan for 30 minutes. Remove from pan and cool completely. Drizzle glaze over.

GLAZE

1 cup confectioners' sugar, sifted
4 tbsp. butter or margarine,
  melted
3 tbsp. orange juice

Mix all ingredients together. Drizzle over cake.

COON HUNTER'S CAKE

2 cups sugar
2 eggs, beaten
½ tsp. baking soda
2 cups self-rising flour
1 tsp. vanilla
1 can (16 oz.) crushed pineapple
  (not drained)
½ cup nuts, chopped

Mix sugar with beaten eggs. Add baking soda to flour. Stir half of flour into sugar-egg mixture. Add vanilla and pineapple. Mix well. Add remaining flour and nuts. Bake in greased and floured 13-by-9-inch pan at 350 degrees for 25 to 30 minutes. Remove from oven. Ice while hot.

ICING

8 oz. cream cheese, softened
½ cup margarine, softened
2 cups confectioners' sugar, sifted
½ cup nuts

Cream together cream cheese and margarine. Add sugar and nuts. Spread on cake.

MOUNTAIN DEW CAKE

4 eggs
1 cup salad oil
1 box orange cake mix
1 box (3 oz.) orange gelatin
1 box (3¼ oz.) coconut pudding
  and pie filling
1 can (12 oz.) Mountain Dew soda

In large mixing bowl, beat eggs well. Mix in oil. Mix together cake mix, gelatin, and pudding mix. Add cake mixture to egg mixture alternately with the Mountain Dew, beginning and ending with cake mix. Divide mixture evenly into three 9-inch greased and floured cake pans. Bake in 350-degree oven for 30 to 35 minutes.

ICING
5 tbsp. flour
2 cups sugar
1 can (20 oz.) crushed pineapple
1 can (8 oz.) crushed pineapple
½ cup butter or margarine
2 cups coconut flakes

Mix flour into sugar. Place all of pineapple in heavy saucepan. Mix in flour-sugar mixture. Cook over medium heat until mixture thickens, about 8 minutes, stirring often. Remove from heat. Add butter and coconut. Spread between cooled cake layers.

OATMEAL CAKE

1½ cups boiling water
1 cup regular oats, uncooked
¼ cup butter or margarine,
   softened
1 cup firmly packed brown sugar
1 cup white sugar
2 eggs, slightly beaten
1 tsp. baking soda
1 tsp. salt
1 tsp. cinnamon
1½ cups flour
1 tsp. vanilla

Pour boiling water over oats. Let stand 20 minutes. Cream butter. Gradually add brown sugar and white sugar, beating well. Stir in oats and eggs. Add baking soda, salt, and cinnamon to flour. Stir into oat mixture. Add vanilla and mix well. Pour into a greased 13-by-9-inch pan. Bake in 350-degree oven for 40 minutes, or until a pick inserted in center comes out clean. Remove from oven and set aside.

TOPPING

1 cup coconut flakes
½ cup pecans, chopped
½ cup butter or margarine, melted
½ cup brown sugar
¼ cup milk
¼ tsp. vanilla

Combine coconut and pecans. Sprinkle over cake. Combine melted butter, brown sugar, milk, and vanilla. Pour over cake. Return to oven. Turn oven to broil and cook 1 to 2 minutes, or until golden brown. Cut in squares to serve.

ORANGE CHIFFON CAKE

2½ cups cake flour
1 tbsp. baking powder
1 tsp. salt
1⅓ cups sugar, divided
½ cup oil
3 egg yolks, beaten
2 tbsp. grated orange rind
¾ cup orange juice
5 egg whites
½ tsp. cream of tartar

Sift together flour, baking powder, salt, and ⅔ cup sugar. Make a well in center. Add oil, egg yolks, orange rind, and juice. Beat on high speed with mixer until all flour is worked in and batter is smooth. Beat egg whites until frothy. Add cream of tartar and beat until soft peaks form. Add remaining ⅔ cup sugar 2 tablespoons at a time, beating well after each addition.

Pour egg yolk batter in a thin stream over egg whites. Gently fold mixtures together. Pour batter into ungreased 10-inch tube pan. Bake in 325-degree oven for 1 hour, or until cake springs back when lightly touched. Cool in pan for 40 minutes. Run knife around sides of pan. Remove cake to plate. Drizzle with orange glaze.

ORANGE GLAZE

3 cups sifted confectioners' sugar
2 tsp. grated orange rind
4 tbsp. orange juice

Combine all ingredients. Drizzle over cake.

PETITS FOURS
(Party Cakes)

4 tbsp. butter or margarine
4 tbsp. shortening
1 cup sugar
½ tsp. vanilla
2 cups cake flour
¼ tsp. salt
3 tsp. baking powder
¾ cup milk
¾ cup egg whites
¼ cup sugar

Grease a 9-by-12-inch baking pan. Line with waxed paper. Grease the paper. Cream together butter, shortening, and 1 cup sugar. Add vanilla. Sift together flour, salt, and baking powder. Add alternately with milk to creamed mixture. Beat egg whites until stiff. Beat in the ¼ cup sugar. Fold egg white mixture into batter.

Pour into prepared pan. Bake in 350-degree oven for 40 minutes, or until wooden pick inserted in center comes out clean. Cool in pan for 5 minutes. Turn out on cake rack to cool. Cut into desired shapes, such as diamonds or squares. Ice each cake separately with petits fours icing. You may want to decorate tops.

PETITS FOURS ICING

2 cups sugar
⅛ tsp. cream of tartar
1 cup hot water
½ tsp. vanilla
1½ cups sifted confectioners'
sugar
Food coloring, if desired

Combine sugar, cream of tartar, and hot water in heavy saucepan. Let come to a boil. Boil until a thin syrup forms or mixture registers 226 degrees on candy thermometer. Remove from heat. Cool to lukewarm. Add vanilla and beat in confectioners' sugar until right consistency to pour. Pour small amounts of icing into other bowls and tint different pastel colors. Ice cakes.

ZUCCHINI CAKE

3 eggs
2 cups sugar
1 cup oil
2 cups grated zucchini squash
2 cups self-rising flour
3 tsp. cinnamon
1 tsp. vanilla
1 cup nuts

Beat eggs. Mix in sugar, oil, zucchini, and flour. Add remaining ingredients. Bake in 13-by-9-inch pan for 45 to 50 minutes in 350-degree oven. Pour on glaze when cake is cooled.

GLAZE

¼ cup margarine or butter
¼ cup buttermilk
1 tsp. white Karo syrup
½ tsp. vanilla

Mix ingredients and heat to boiling. Pour on cooled cake.

LANE CAKE

Although this cake was not named in relation to Grandpapa and Grandmama Lane, our family always felt a special kinship with it.

1 cup butter or margarine,
   softened
2 cups sugar
3¼ cups all-purpose flour
1 tbsp. baking powder
¾ tsp. salt
1 cup milk
1 tsp. vanilla
8 egg whites, stiffly beaten

Cream together the butter and sugar. Sift together flour, baking powder, and salt. Add to creamed mixture alternately with milk, beginning and ending with flour. Mix well after each addition. Stir in vanilla. Fold in stiffly beaten egg whites.

Pour batter into three greased and flour-dusted 9-inch cake pans. Bake in 325-degree oven for 25 minutes, or until wooden pick inserted in center comes out clean. Cool in pans for 10 minutes. Remove from pans and cool completely. Prepare filling.

FILLING

8 egg yolks
1½ cups sugar
½ cup butter or margarine
1 cup chopped pecans
1 cup golden raisins
1 cup coconut flakes
¼ cup bourbon or orange juice
½ cup chopped maraschino
   cherries

Combine beaten egg yolks, sugar, and butter in heavy saucepan. Cook over medium heat, stirring constantly until thickened, about 20 minutes. Remove from heat. Stir in remaining ingredients. Cool. Spread between layers and on top of cake. Spread sides of cake with icing.

ICING

2 egg whites
½ cup white corn syrup
½ cup sugar
⅛ tsp. salt
1 tsp. vanilla

Combine egg whites, syrup, sugar, and salt in top of double boiler. Beat with mixer just until combined. Sit over rapidly boiling water. Cook, beating constantly until icing stands in stiff peaks. Remove from hot water. Add vanilla. Beat another minute or two. Cover sides of Lane Cake with icing.

BASIC PIE CRUST

½ cup shortening
1½ cups self-rising flour
4 to 5 tbsp. ice water

Cut shortening into flour with pastry blender until consistency of coarse meal. Add water a little at a time until all flour is moistened. Roll out on floured surface to fit pie pan. To bake, prick with fork and bake in 400-degree oven for 10 minutes, or until brown. Makes enough dough for two 9-inch crusts.

SWEET VELVET CAKE

1 cup oil
1½ cups sugar
3 eggs
2½ cups flour
1 tsp. baking soda
¼ tsp. salt
2 tbsp. cocoa
1 cup buttermilk
1 tsp. vanilla
1 bottle (1 oz.) red food coloring

Cream oil and sugar. Add eggs one at a time, beating well after each addition. Sift together flour, baking soda, salt, and cocoa. Add alternately with buttermilk to egg mixture. Add vanilla and food coloring. Beat until smooth. Pour into two greased and floured cake pans. Bake in 350-degree oven for 25 to 30 minutes. Cool completely before icing.

ICING

½ cup butter or margarine,
softened
8 oz. cream cheese, softened
1 box (1 lb.) confectioners' sugar
1 cup whipped cream
1 cup pecans, finely chopped

Beat together butter and cream cheese. Add sifted confectioners' sugar. Add whipped cream. Mix well. Add pecans. Spread between layers and on top and sides of cold cake.

APPLE PIE

⅔ cup sugar
1 tbsp. cornstarch
½ tsp. cinnamon
¼ tsp. salt
6 cups thinly sliced, peeled tart
  apples
4 tbsp. melted butter

Mix sugar, cornstarch, cinnamon, and salt. Mix with apples. Put into pastry-lined deep dish pie pan. Pour melted butter over all. Cover with top crust. Bake at 350 degrees about 50 minutes, or until crust is brown.

DUTCH APPLE PIE

1 unbaked 9-inch deep-dish pie
  shell
5 cups peeled and chopped apples
½ cup sugar
¼ tsp. salt
½ tsp. cinnamon
⅓ cup brown sugar
⅔ cup self-rising flour
6 tbsp. butter or margarine

Place apples in pie shell. Mix sugar, salt, and cinnamon together. Sprinkle over apples. In mixing bowl, stir brown sugar into flour. With pastry blender or two knives, cut in butter until crumbly. Sprinkle over apples. Bake in 350-degree oven for 40 to 45 minutes, or until top is brown and filling is bubbling. Serve warm with ice cream.

AUNT CLARA'S LEMON CHESS PIE

4 eggs
1 tbsp. flour
1 tbsp. cornmeal
2 cups sugar
¼ cup milk
½ cup lemon juice
¼ cup butter or margarine, melted
1 tbsp. grated lemon peel
1 deep-dish unbaked pie crust

In large mixing bowl, beat eggs. Mix flour and cornmeal with sugar. Add to eggs, mixing well. Stir in milk, lemon juice, melted butter, and lemon peel. Pour into unbaked pie shell. Bake in 350-degree oven for 45 minutes, or until brown and set.

PLAIN OLD-FASHIONED CHESS PIE

1½ cups sugar
1 tbsp. flour
1 tbsp. cornmeal
2 eggs
4 tbsp. melted butter
½ cup milk or cream
½ tsp. vanilla
1 unbaked pie shell

Mix sugar, flour, and cornmeal. Add beaten eggs, butter, milk, and vanilla. Pour in unbaked pie shell. Bake at 350 degrees for 45 minutes, or until very brown and set.

BLACK BOTTOM PIE

2 tbsp. cornstarch
1¼ cups sugar
3 cups milk
6 egg yolks, beaten
1 tsp. vanilla
2 squares unsweetened chocolate,
  melted
1 baked 9-inch pie crust
1 envelope unflavored gelatin
¼ cup cold water
3 tbsp. rum
4 egg whites
Whipped cream
Chocolate sprinkles

In heavy saucepan, combine cornstarch and ¾ cup sugar. Stir in milk. Cook over low heat, stirring constantly until thickened (8 to 10 minutes). Blend a small amount into beaten egg yolks. Pour all back into saucepan. Cook 2 minutes longer, stirring constantly. Remove from heat.

Stir in vanilla. Measure out 2 cups of the custard. Stir chocolate into these 2 cups of custard. Cool. Pour into baked crust. Soften gelatin in water. Add to remaining custard. Stir in rum. Cool, stirring often until thickened. Beat egg whites until stiff. Beat in remaining ½ cup sugar. Fold into chilled gelatin mixture. Spoon over chocolate in pie shell. Chill several hours, preferably overnight. Garnish with whipped cream and chocolate sprinkles.

CARAMEL PIE

2 cups sugar
⅓ cup flour
1½ cups milk
3 eggs
1 tsp. vanilla
4 tbsp. butter or margarine
1 baked pie crust

In heavy saucepan, mix 1 cup sugar and the flour together. Add milk, stirring to blend. Place on medium heat. Cook, stirring until mixture begins to thicken, about 3 minutes. Separate eggs, beat yolks, and add about 1 cup of hot mixture to yolks. Mix yolks into mixture in saucepan. Continue to cook, stirring constantly until thickened, 5 to 8 minutes.

Meanwhile, place 1 cup sugar in heavy skillet. Melt over medium heat until brown. Add to hot mixture, blending together until smooth. Remove from heat. Add vanilla and butter. Cool while preparing meringue. Pour into baked pie crust. Top with meringue.

MERINGUE

3 egg whites
¼ tsp. cream of tartar
6 tbsp. sugar
½ tsp. vanilla

Beat egg whites with cream of tartar until soft peaks form. Gradually add sugar, beating well. Add vanilla. Spread over pie filling. Bake in 350-degree oven for 10 to 15 minutes, until brown.

CHOCOLATE CHIP WALNUT PIE

Black walnuts being so hard to come by, wouldn't you say a gift of one quart of black walnuts would be the most memorable gift one could ever receive? I once received this gift and felt very unworthy. It must have taken my dear friend Mickey hours to burst those hard shells and pick out the nuts. How could I possibly make a dessert worthy of those nuts?

Having saved them for months, at Christmastime I decided I must use them or they would become stale. After I made Chocolate Chip Walnut Pie, Divinity Candy, and Mickey's Christmas Cookies, all my precious walnuts were gone. The recipe for Divinity Candy and Mickey's Christmas Cookies can be found in the next chapter. Now, here's Chocolate Chip Walnut Pie.

3 eggs
⅛ tsp. salt
1 cup sugar
1 cup white corn syrup
¼ cup butter or margarine, melted
1 cup semisweet chocolate chips
1 tsp. vanilla
1 cup chopped black walnuts
One 9-inch unbaked pie shell

Beat eggs. Blend in salt, sugar, syrup, and butter. Stir in chips, vanilla, and walnuts. Pour into pie shell. Bake in 350-degree oven for 45 minutes, or until set and brown.

MAMA'S EASY CHOCOLATE PIE

1½ cups sugar
⅓ cup cocoa
½ cup self-rising flour
1½ cups milk
2 eggs, separated
4 tbsp. butter
½ tsp. vanilla
4 tbsp. sugar
½ tsp. vanilla
1 baked pie shell

Mix 1½ cups sugar, cocoa, and flour in heavy saucepan. Add milk. Cook over low heat, stirring occasionally until hot. Beat egg yolks. Add about 1 cup of hot pie mixture to egg yolks. Pour back into hot cocoa mix in saucepan. Cook, stirring often till mixture is thick (5 to 8 minutes).

Remove from heat. Add butter and ½ tsp. vanilla. Beat till smooth. Set aside to cool while preparing meringue. For meringue, beat egg whites until stiff. Add 4 tbsp. sugar one tablespoon at a time, beating to combine. Add ½ tsp. vanilla. Pour chocolate mixture into baked pie shell. Top with egg whites. Brown in 350-degree oven for 10 to 15 minutes. Great served with vanilla ice cream while hot.

BUTTERMILK PIE

2 tbsp. flour
2 cups sugar
½ cup butter, softened
4 eggs
⅔ cup buttermilk
⅛ tsp. salt
1 tsp. vanilla
2 unbaked 9-inch pie crusts

Mix flour into sugar. Cream sugar and flour mixture into butter. Add eggs one at a time, beating well after each addition. Add buttermilk, salt, and vanilla. Divide mixture evenly between 2 unbaked pie shells. Bake in 325-degree oven for 40 minutes, or until brown and set.

COCONUT CREAM PIE

1½ cups sugar
3 tbsp. cornstarch
1½ cups milk
3 eggs, separated
4 tbsp. butter or margarine
1 tsp. vanilla
1¼ cups coconut flakes
1 baked 9-inch pie shell

In heavy saucepan or top of double boiler, mix sugar and corn-starch. Add milk, stirring to mix thoroughly. Place over medium heat and cook until mixture is hot. Beat egg yolks. Add about 1 cup of hot mixture to egg yolks. Pour into custard. Cook until thickened, 10 to 15 minutes.

Add butter or margarine. Stir until butter melts. Remove from heat. Add vanilla and 1 cup coconut. Let cool while preparing meringue. Beat egg whites until stiff. Add 6 tbsp. sugar a little at a time, beating well after each addition. Add 1 tsp. vanilla.

Pour filling into baked pie shell. Top with meringue. Sprinkle ¼ cup coconut over meringue. Put in 350-degree oven. Bake 10 to 15 minutes, or until brown. To make banana cream pie add 2 sliced bananas instead of coconut.

FRIED PIES

Everyone was in bed when there was a knock on the door. Papa called out, "Who's there?"

"It's Big John, Mr. Joge. I's hongry, broke, and froze."

"Are you drunk, John?"

"No suh, Mr. Joge. Jest don't thank I kin make it on home tonight. If'n I could sleep in ye hayloft I'd be muchablidge."

"Well, come on in the house, John, and get warm."

"Who is it, George?"

"It's John, Eva. He's hungry and wants to spend the night in the barn."

"There's fried pies in the pie safe. Give 'im a quart of milk to wash 'em down. Quilts and a pillow in the quilt box."

Come morning, Papa went out to get Big John for breakfast, but he had gone, the quilts left folded neatly in the hayloft.

⅓ cup shortening
1½ cups self-rising flour
⅓ cup ice water
Oil

Cut shortening into flour, using knives or pastry blender. Add ice water. If not enough to combine flour, add more water 1 teaspoon at a time. On lightly floured surface roll out thin. Cut into 6-inch rounds. Place 2 tablespoons filling in center of each round. Moisten edges. Fold over and press edges together with fingers or tines of fork. Fry in 2-inch-deep hot oil, turning to brown on both sides, about 3 minutes per side. Drain on paper towels.

CHOCOLATE FILLING

¼ cup sugar
¼ cup self-rising flour
1 tbsp. cocoa powder
½ cup milk
2 tbsp. butter or margarine
½ tsp. vanilla

In heavy saucepan, combine sugar, flour, and cocoa. Stir in milk and butter. Cook over medium heat, stirring constantly until thickened and smooth (3 to 5 minutes). Remove from heat. Stir in vanilla. Cool completely before making pies.

ANOTHER CHOCOLATE FILLING

2 tbsp. cocoa powder
½ cup sugar
¼ cup melted butter or margarine

Mix cocoa and sugar together. Sprinkle 2 teaspoons of mixture on crust round. Drizzle with 2 teaspoons butter. Proceed as directed above.

FRIED PEACH PIES

2 cups dried peaches (7-oz. pkg.)
1¾ cups water
½ cup sugar, or to taste
¼ cup butter or margarine

Wash peaches. Cover with water. Bring to a boil, and boil 15 minutes. Add sugar. Cook 5 more minutes, stirring often to prevent sticking. Remove from heat. Add butter. When cooled, place 2 tablespoons peaches on pie crust round and proceed as directed above.

Note: For Fried Apple Pies, just substitute apples for peaches.

LEMON MERINGUE PIE

1⅓ cups sugar
¼ cup cornstarch
¼ tsp. salt
1¾ cups water
**4 egg yolks (save whites for
  meringue)**
2 tbsp. butter
1 tbsp. grated lemon rind
½ cup lemon juice
1 baked pie shell

Combine sugar, cornstarch, and salt in heavy saucepan or double boiler. Add water. Cook, stirring often until boiling and thickened, 5 to 8 minutes. Beat egg yolks. Blend into ½ cup of hot mixture. Slowly stir into mixture in pan. Cook 2 minutes. Stir in butter, lemon rind, and lemon juice. Remove from heat. Set aside to cool while making meringue.

MERINGUE

4 egg whites
¼ tsp. cream of tartar
½ cup sugar
½ tsp. vanilla extract
½ tsp. lemon extract

Beat egg whites and cream of tartar until stiff peaks form. Slowly add sugar, beating as it is added. Add extracts. Pour pie filling in baked shell. Top with meringue. Put in 350-degree oven for 10 to 15 minutes, or until meringue is brown.

FRESH STRAWBERRY PIE

1½ qt. fresh strawberries
3 tbsp. cornstarch
1 cup sugar
1 tbsp. butter
1 baked 9-inch pie crust or
  graham cracker crust
1 carton (8 oz.) whipped topping

Wash and cap berries. Set aside half of them. Mash remaining berries. Add cornstarch to sugar. Stir into mashed berries. Add butter. Cook in heavy saucepan until clear and thick, about 5 minutes. Cool. Save a few whole berries for garnish. Slice remaining ones into bottom of pie crust, or you can leave whole. Pour in cooked berries. When cooled, spread with whipped topping. Garnish with whole berries.

SWEET POTATO PIE

2 cups cooked and mashed sweet
  potatoes
2 cups sugar
3 eggs, beaten
⅔ cup evaporated milk
½ cup butter or margarine, melted
1 tsp. vanilla
½ tsp. cinnamon
2 unbaked pie shells

Mix sweet potatoes and remaining filling ingredients together. Divide evenly into 2 pie shells. Bake in 350-degree oven for 45 to 50 minutes, or until set and brown.

MAMA'S EGG CUSTARD PIE

3 eggs
½ cup sugar
¼ tsp. salt
2 cups milk
1 tsp. vanilla
1 unbaked 9-inch pie shell

Preheat oven to 425 degrees. Beat eggs until thoroughly blended. Add sugar, salt, milk, and vanilla, stirring until smooth. Pour into pie shell. Bake at 425 degrees for 15 minutes. Reduce oven temperature to 350 degrees. Bake about 30 minutes longer, until knife inserted about 1 inch from edge of pan comes out clean. Cool before serving.

SOUTHERN PECAN PIE

3 eggs
1 cup sugar
1 cup dark corn syrup
⅓ cup melted butter
1 tsp. vanilla
1 cup pecans
1 unbaked pie shell

Beat eggs. Beat in sugar, syrup, butter, and vanilla. Fold in pecans. Pour into unbaked pie shell. Bake in 325-degree oven for 50 to 55 minutes, until brown and set.

CRACKER PIE

3 egg whites
1 tsp. cream of tartar
1 cup sugar
16 soda crackers, crumbled
1 cup chopped nuts
2 tbsp. pineapple preserves
1 container (8 oz.) whipped
   topping

Beat the egg whites and cream of tartar until stiff. Add sugar and beat well. Mix in cracker crumbs and chopped nuts. Pour into buttered 9-inch pie pan. Bake in 350-degree oven for 25 minutes. Spread pineapple preserves on top. Cool and serve with whipped topping.

PINTO BEAN PIE

1 egg
½ cup brown sugar
¾ cup white sugar
½ cup butter or margarine, melted
½ cup coconut flakes
½ cup mashed pinto beans
½ tsp. vanilla
1 unbaked pie shell

Beat egg. Add sugar and melted butter. Stir in coconut, beans, and vanilla. Pour into unbaked pie shell. Bake in 325-degree oven for 40 to 45 minutes.

GREEN TOMATO PIE

When I was growing up, at the first hint of frost all green tomatoes were picked and put in the root cellar. Some were wrapped in newspaper and placed in a bushel basket, to be taken out from time to time and put on the windowsill in the kitchen to ripen. We would sometimes have ripe tomatoes clean up till Christmas. Some were used to make Green Tomato Pie, Fried Green Tomatoes, and Green Tomato Relish. This is Mama's Green Tomato Pie recipe. The other two recipes can be found elsewhere in this book.

> **8 green tomatoes (about 3½ lb.),
>   diced
> 1 cup raisins
> 1 cup brown sugar
> ¼ cup butter or margarine
> ¼ cup red wine vinegar
> 1 tsp. vanilla
> ½ tsp. cinnamon
> ½ tsp. allspice
> Enough pie pastry for 2 pies**

Place tomatoes, raisins, brown sugar, butter, and vinegar in heavy saucepan. Mix well. Put on medium heat. Bring to a boil, then turn heat down to simmer. Cook about 1 hour until very thick, stirring occasionally. Remove from heat. Add vanilla, cinnamon, and allspice. Cool. Prepare pastry. Pour mixture into 1 pastry-lined pan. Cover with remaining pastry lattice-style. Brush with melted butter. Bake in 350-degree oven for 45 minutes, or until crust is brown.

Cookies, Candies, and Other Desserts

Sorghum cane being fed into the press mill to squeeze out the juice for making sorghum molasses.

ALMOND BUTTER COOKIES

**1 cup butter or margarine,
  softened
1 cup sugar
2 egg yolks
½ tsp. almond extract
2 cups all-purpose flour
1 tsp. baking powder
¼ tsp. salt
½ cup whole almonds**

Cream butter and sugar together. Beat in egg yolks and almond extract. Sift together flour, baking powder, and salt. Stir into butter mixture. Shape dough into 1-inch balls. Place 2 inches apart on ungreased cookie sheet. Press almond in center of each cookie. Bake in 300-degree oven for 15 to 20 minutes, or until edges of cookies begin to brown. Cool 5 minutes before removing from cookie sheet. Makes about 3 dozen.

CRISP NUT SLICES

**½ cup butter or margarine,
  softened
½ cup sugar
1 tbsp. molasses
⅛ tsp. salt
½ cup chopped nuts
1½ cups flour
½ tsp. baking soda**

Cream together butter, sugar, molasses, and salt. Stir in nuts. Sift together flour and baking soda. Stir into creamed mixture. Shape dough into a 10-inch roll. Wrap in plastic wrap and refrigerate 1 hour or longer. When ready to bake, slice in thin slices and bake on greased cookie sheet in 350-degree oven for 8 to 10 minutes, or until light brown. Makes about 40.

CHOCOLATE CHIP COOKIES

**1 cup butter or margarine,
    softened**
¾ cup sugar
¾ cup brown sugar
1 tsp. vanilla
2 eggs
2¼ cups flour
1 tsp. baking soda
½ tsp. salt
**1½ cups semisweet chocolate
    chips**

Cream butter, sugars, and vanilla until light and fluffy. Add eggs, beating well. Combine flour, baking soda, and salt. Gradually stir into creamed mixture. Stir in chocolate chips. Drop by teaspoonfuls onto ungreased cookie sheet. Bake in 375-degree oven for 8 to 10 minutes, or until light brown. Makes about 6 dozen.

FUN FUN FORTUNE COOKIES

Here are some suggested fortunes. You may want to write your own to suit your guests.

"Don't marry for money. You can borrow it cheaper."
"This is your unlucky day. Crawl in a hole and pull the hole in after you."
"Love is a two-way street. You are on a one-way traveling in the wrong direction."
"Marilyn Monroe you are not, but you do have savoir-faire."
"You are no Clark Gable, but you do give a damn."
"Your highway to Heaven is your favorite fishing stream."
"Don't despair; beauty is only skin deep. Your beauty lies within."
"Problems are a dime a dozen. If you could sell yours, you would be rich."
"You do too have sense enough to come in out of the rain. You've done it lots of times."
"Some folks got it and some ain't. You know if you got it or you ain't."
"Only a dummy would believe a fortune in a fortune cookie."

**3 tbsp. butter or margarine,
    softened
3 tbsp. sugar
1 egg white
½ tsp. vanilla
⅛ tsp. salt
⅓ cup flour**

Grease cookie sheet. Dip 3-inch cookie cutter or glass in flour. Press 6 outlines firmly 1 inch apart on prepared cookie sheet. Set aside. Beat together butter, sugar, egg white, and vanilla. Mix salt into flour. Stir into butter-sugar-egg mixture until well blended.

With spatula, spread rounded teaspoonful of batter in each outlined circle on cookie sheet. Bake in preheated 400-degree oven for 4 to 5 minutes, or until edges of cookies are light brown. Remove from oven. Quickly loosen cookies with spatula. Turn bottom-side up.

Place folded fortune in center. Gently fold cookie in half, holding edges together to the count of 3. Place center of fold over rim of glass. Gently press ends down to bend cookie in middle. Let cool. Repeat with remaining cookies. If cookies become too brittle to fold, return to oven briefly to soften. Makes about 20 cookies.

MAMA'S TEA CAKES

1 cup butter or margarine,
　softened
2 cups sugar
3 eggs
2 tbsp. buttermilk
5 cups self-rising flour
¼ tsp. baking soda
1 tsp. vanilla
Additional sugar

Cream butter. Gradually add sugar, beating well. Add eggs one at a time, beating well after each addition. Add buttermilk and beat well. Combine flour and baking soda and gradually stir into cream mixture. Add vanilla and stir. Chill dough in refrigerator for 1 hour or more.

Roll dough to ¼-inch thickness on lightly floured surface. Cut with biscuit cutter. Place 1 inch apart on lightly greased cookie sheets. Sprinkle with sugar. Bake at 350 degrees for 7 to 8 minutes, or until edges are light brown. Remove to wire racks to cool. Makes about 4 dozen.

CRUNCHY OATMEAL COOKIES

1 cup all-purpose flour
½ tsp. baking soda
½ cup firmly packed brown sugar
½ cup white sugar
½ cup shortening
1 egg
½ tsp. vanilla
1 cup crushed cornflakes
1 cup oats

Sift together flour and baking soda. Set aside. Cream together sugars and shortening. Blend in egg and vanilla. Add flour. Mix well. Stir in cornflakes and oats. Shape by teaspoonfuls into balls. Place on greased cookie sheets. Flatten with bottom of glass dipped in flour. Bake at 350 degrees for 8 to 10 minutes. Makes 3 to 4 dozen.

IRENE'S PEANUT BUTTER COOKIES

1 cup margarine, softened
1 cup white sugar
1 cup brown sugar
2 eggs, well beaten
1 tsp. vanilla
½ tsp. baking soda
1¼ cups self-rising flour
1 cup peanut butter

Cream margarine and sugars. Add eggs and vanilla. Add baking soda to flour. Mix into egg mixture. Add peanut butter. Roll into small balls. Place on ungreased cookie sheet. Bake in 375-degree oven for 10 minutes, or until brown. Makes 3 to 4 dozen.

MS. PEARL'S HONEY KRINKLES

1 cup sugar
⅔ cup oil
¼ cup honey
1 egg
1 tsp. ginger
2 cups self-rising flour

Mix ½ cup sugar, oil, and honey together. Beat in egg. Add ginger to flour. Stir into sugar mixture. Place remaining ½ cup sugar in shallow bowl. Drop dough by teaspoons into sugar, rolling over to coat. Place on greased cookie sheet. Bake in 350-degree oven for 7 to 10 minutes. Makes 3 to 4 dozen.

PERSIMMON COOKIES

½ cup butter or margarine
1 cup sugar
1 egg
1 cup persimmon pulp
2 cups flour
1 tsp. baking soda
¼ tsp. salt
¼ tsp. cinnamon
½ tsp. allspice
1 cup chopped nuts

Preheat oven to 350 degrees. Cream together butter and sugar. Beat in egg. Stir in persimmon pulp. Sift together flour, baking soda, salt, and spices. Add to butter-sugar mixture. Stir in nuts. Drop by teaspoonfuls onto greased baking sheet. Bake 10 to 12 minutes, or until lightly browned. Makes about 3 dozen.

MICKEY'S CHRISTMAS COOKIES

1½ cups firmly packed brown
   sugar
1 cup butter or margarine
2 eggs, beaten
2½ cups flour
1 tsp. salt
1 tsp. cinnamon
1 tsp. baking soda, dissolved in
   small amount of water
½ tsp. vanilla
1 lb. dates, chopped
1 lb. candied cherries, chopped
½ lb. candied pineapple, chopped
2 cups pecans, coarsely chopped
2 cups Brazil nuts, coarsely
   chopped

Cream together brown sugar and butter. Add eggs, mixing well. Mix together flour, salt, and cinnamon. Add to egg mixture. Add baking soda and vanilla. Dough will be stiff. Add fruit and nuts. Drop by teaspoon onto greased cookie sheets. Bake in 325-degree oven for 15 to 20 minutes. This dough will keep for weeks in the refrigerator if you don't want to make all the cookies at one time. Makes 5 dozen.

PUMPKIN COOKIE BARS

1 cup flour
½ cup quick cooking oats
½ cup firmly packed brown sugar
½ cup chopped nuts
1 tsp. cinnamon
½ cup melted butter or margarine
1 cup canned pumpkin

¾ cup undiluted evaporated milk
1 egg, beaten
⅓ cup sugar
½ tsp. allspice

Combine flour, oats, brown sugar, nuts, and cinnamon. Add butter and mix well. Press into bottom of 13-by-9-inch baking pan. Bake in 350-degree oven for 20 to 25 minutes. Remove from oven. Reduce oven temperature to 325 degrees. Combine remaining ingredients. Pour over crust. Bake in 325-degree oven for 25 to 30 minutes, or until wooden pick inserted in center comes out clean. Cool and ice.

ICING

8 oz. cream cheese, softened
¼ cup orange marmalade
½ cup chopped nuts

Beat cream cheese until smooth. Beat in marmalade. Stir in nuts. Spread on cooled pumpkin cookie bars. Makes 24 2-inch bars.

POTATO CANDY

½ cup cooked mashed potatoes
2 boxes (1 lb. each) confectioners'
   sugar
1 tsp. vanilla
1 cup peanut butter

Mix potatoes, sifted confectioners' sugar, and vanilla together. Roll out about ¼ inch thick. Spread with peanut butter. Roll up like jelly roll. To serve, slice in ¼- to ½-inch pieces. Makes about 2¼ pounds.

REFRIGERATOR COOKIES

1 cup butter or margarine,
  softened
1½ cups sugar
2 eggs
1 tsp. vanilla
3 cups flour
2 tsp. baking powder
½ tsp. salt

Cream together butter and sugar. Beat in eggs and vanilla. Sift flour, baking powder, and salt together. Add to cream mixture. Chill dough in refrigerator for 1 hour. Form into 3 rolls 9 inches long. Wrap in plastic wrap and keep in refrigerator. When ready to bake, slice in ⅛- to ¼-inch pieces. Place about 1 inch apart on lightly greased cookie sheet. Bake in 375-degree oven for 10 minutes, or until lightly brown. Makes 8 to 10 dozen.

Variations: For lemon cookies, substitute 2 teaspoons lemon extract for vanilla.
For nut cookies, add ½ cup chopped nuts to dough.
For spice cookies, add ½ teaspoon cinnamon and ½ teaspoon nutmeg to dough.

DIVINITY CANDY

2 cups sugar
½ cup white corn syrup
½ cup water
2 egg whites
1 tsp. vanilla
1 cup chopped nuts

In heavy saucepan, mix together sugar, corn syrup, and water. Cover pan and boil 3 minutes, without stirring to dissolve crystals. Remove lid and continue boiling until mixture reaches soft-ball stage, or 240 degrees on candy thermometer. Remove from heat.

While sugar mixture is boiling, beat egg whites until stiff. Immediately after removing sugar mixture from heat, pour in a thin stream over beaten egg whites, beating constantly. Beat in vanilla, and continue to beat until candy cools and begins to get stiff. Fold in nuts.

Drop by spoonfuls onto waxed paper. Food coloring may be added to make different colors, or you can add red or green candied cherries. This is a very pretty candy, as well as a delicious one. Makes about 1½ dozen pieces.

TAFFY

2 cups light corn syrup
1 cup sugar
2 tbsp. vinegar
¼ tsp. baking soda
1 tsp. vanilla

Combine syrup, sugar, and vinegar in 3-quart saucepan. Bring to a boil, stirring constantly until sugar dissolves. After 10 minutes, start testing for hard-ball stage by dropping small amount in very cold water. Continue cooking to hard-ball stage, 250 to 260 degrees on candy thermometer.

Remove from heat and stir in baking soda and vanilla. Beat until smooth and creamy. Pour into buttered pan. When cool enough to handle, pull with buttered hands until satiny and light colored. Pull into a long strip and cut into 1-inch pieces with scissors. Makes about 1 pound or 80 pieces.

PEANUT BRITTLE

2 cups sugar
½ cup water
⅔ cup white syrup
2 cups raw peanuts
2 tbsp. butter
2 tsp. baking soda
1 tsp. vanilla

Combine sugar, water, and syrup. Cook without stirring until mixture spins a thread when poured from a spoon. Add peanuts and butter. Continue to cook till golden brown. Remove from heat quickly, then stir in baking soda and vanilla. Pour in buttered pan. When cool, break in pieces. Makes about 2 pounds.

PECAN PRALINES

1 cup buttermilk
1 tsp. baking soda
2 cups sugar
2 cups pecans
1 tbsp. butter
1 tsp. vanilla

Mix in heavy saucepan buttermilk, baking soda, and sugar. Cook over medium heat, stirring constantly to soft-ball stage. Mixture will turn brown. Remove from heat. Add pecans, butter, and vanilla. Drop by teaspoon on wax paper. Makes about 3 dozen.

APPLE FRITTERS

1 egg
⅓ cup sugar
1 cup milk
3 tbsp. orange juice
1 cup unpeeled, finely chopped
   apple
½ tsp. vanilla
2 cups self-rising flour
Hot oil
Sifted confectioners' sugar

Beat egg. Add sugar. Slowly stir in milk and orange juice. Blend in apple, vanilla, and flour. Drop mixture by teaspoonfuls into hot oil. Fry until brown on both sides, about 3 minutes per side. Drain in colander or on paper towels. Dust with confectioners' sugar. Makes 4 dozen.

QUICKIE PEACH COBBLER

½ cup butter or margarine
1 can (1 lb. 14 oz.) sliced
   peaches, drained
1 cup sugar
1 cup self-rising flour
¾ cup juice from peaches

Put butter in 2-quart baking dish in 350-degree oven until melted. Remove from oven. Add drained peaches. Do not stir. Mix sugar, flour, and juice until smooth. Pour over peaches. Do not stir. Bake in 350-degree oven for 45 to 50 minutes, or until set and brown. Serve hot with ice cream. Serves 6 to 8.

MAMA'S WILD
BLACKBERRY COBBLER

5 cups blackberries
1½ cups sugar
1 tbsp. cornstarch
4 tbsp. butter

Place blackberries in 8- or 9-inch baking pan. Mix sugar and corn-starch together. Sprinkle over berries. Dot with butter. Set aside and make crust.

CRUST

½ cup shortening
1½ cups self-rising flour
¼ cup ice water, or more if
 needed
4 tbsp. butter
2 tbsp. sugar

Cut shortening into flour. Add ice water until mixture is well moist-ened and holds together. Roll out on floured surface. Fit over berries. Dot with butter. Sprinkle with sugar. Bake in 350-degree oven for 40 to 45 minutes, until crust is brown. Serves 6 to 8.

HONEY AMBROSIA

4 oranges, peeled, seeded, and
  chopped
3 bananas, peeled and sliced
½ cup flaked coconut
½ cup orange juice
¼ cup honey
1 tbsp. lemon juice

Combine fruit and coconut. Mix orange juice, honey, and lemon juice. Pour over fruit and mix well. Serves 8.

RICE PUDDING

1½ cups milk
⅛ tsp. salt
⅓ cup sugar
1 tbsp. butter, melted
5 eggs, beaten
¼ cup peach brandy
2 cups cooked rice
1 tbsp. lemon juice
¼ tsp. nutmeg

Mix together thoroughly the first 6 ingredients. Stir in rice and lemon juice. Pour into a greased 2-quart baking dish. Sprinkle top with nutmeg. Bake in 325-degree oven for 50 minutes, or until light brown and set. Test by sticking table knife in center of dish. If knife comes out clean, pudding is done. Serve hot or cold. Serves 8.

BANANA PUDDING

Bananas were a real treat for us, a treat we only got to enjoy when Papa carried the first bale of cotton to the gin in the fall. His first stop was Mr. Rucker's grocery. He'd settle up and buy candy for everyone, a stalk of bananas, and graham crackers.

All the family loved banana pudding with the exception of me, the finicky eater. The mutilation of all those wonderful bananas for a pudding seemed like such a waste, but Mama always saved two or three for me. The pudding was made in Mama's huge turkey roasting pan. I have since learned to like banana pudding and have scaled down and revised Mama's recipe. She used graham crackers and topped her pudding with meringue. My recipe calls for vanilla wafers, and the egg whites are mixed into the custard, therefore eliminating the baking of the meringue.

Speaking of bananas always brings to mind Mary Ann Garner and her bananas. Being the only one in school whose parents could afford to buy a banana for her lunch sack, she made sure that everyone in school saw her eating it. She would peel it down and take a bite of it during the first recess, at dinner she peeled it down a little more and licked around on it with her long tongue (that girl had the longest tongue I ever did see), and at last recess she finally finished it while all us kids drooled and ached for a bite of banana.

1 cup sugar
2 tbsp. cornstarch
⅛ tsp. salt
3 cups milk
2 eggs, separated
4 tbsp. butter or margarine
½ tsp. vanilla
Vanilla wafers
6 bananas

Combine sugar, cornstarch, and salt in heavy saucepan. Stir in milk. Cook over medium heat, stirring constantly until thickened, about 15 minutes. Beat egg yolks. Stir small amount of hot mixture into egg yolks, then stir yolks into rest of mixture.

Add butter and continue to cook for 5 minutes, stirring constantly. Remove from heat. Beat egg whites until stiff. Stir into hot pudding mixture. Beat until smooth. Add vanilla. Line 2-quart bowl with vanilla wafers. Top with some of the sliced bananas. Pour some of pudding over bananas. Continue layers of wafers, bananas, and pudding mix, ending with pudding on top. Sprinkle top with wafer crumbs. Refrigerate. Serve cold. Serves 8.

MOLASSES PUDDING

My friend Jeanette's grandmother, Mrs. Caralyne Churchwell, gave this recipe to her many years ago. Although it is much like gingerbread, she called it Molasses Pudding.

¼ cup butter
½ cup sugar
1 egg, beaten
1 cup sorghum molasses
2 cups self-rising flour
1 tsp. ginger
1 tsp. cinnamon
½ tsp. baking soda
½ cup buttermilk
1 tsp. vanilla

Cream together butter and sugar. Beat in egg and sorghum. Sift together flour, ginger, and cinnamon. Stir baking soda into buttermilk. Add flour and buttermilk to sorghum mixture. Stir in vanilla. Pour into greased and floured 9-inch square baking pan. Bake in 350-degree oven for 45 to 50 minutes, until brown and firm. Serves 8.

OLD-TIME SWEET POTATO PUDDING

4 cups grated raw sweet potatoes
1 cup sugar
1½ cups evaporated milk
⅓ cup butter or margarine, melted
3 eggs, beaten
1 tsp. nutmeg
1 tsp. cinnamon
½ tsp. salt

Combine all ingredients, mixing well. Grease 2-quart baking dish. Spoon mixture into baking dish. Bake in 325-degree oven for 1½ hours, or until firm. Serves 8.

BISCUIT PUDDING

You can use leftover biscuits for this pudding if you have any.

6 biscuits
¼ cup butter, softened
1 cup sugar
2 eggs
2 cups milk
½ tsp. vanilla

Spread biscuits with softened butter. Arrange half of biscuits, buttered side up, in 9-by-9-by-2-inch baking pan. Sprinkle with ¼ cup sugar. Put remaining half of biscuits on top, buttered side up. Sprinkle with ¼ cup sugar. Set aside. Beat eggs. Add remaining ½ cup sugar, milk, and vanilla. Pour over biscuits. Bake in 350-degree oven for 30 minutes, or until set and brown. Serves 8.

SNOWBALL PUDDINGS IN PEACH SAUCE

¼ cup butter or margarine
½ cup sugar
½ tsp. vanilla
1 egg, beaten
1 cup self-rising flour
¼ cup evaporated milk plus 2
    tbsp. water

Cream together butter and sugar. Beat in vanilla and egg. Add flour to mixture alternately with milk and water. Spoon into greased custard cups, filling ⅔ full. Set in pan containing 1 inch hot water. Cover cups with waxed paper. Bake in 350-degree oven for 35 minutes, or until puddings shrink from sides of cups. Turn out in shallow bowl. Serve warm with peach sauce. Prepare peach sauce while puddings bake.

PEACH SAUCE

2 cups sliced peaches
1 cup juice, drained from peaches
¼ cup sugar
1 tbsp. cornstarch
½ tsp. salt
2 tbsp. butter
1 cup evaporated milk

Drain juice from peaches. If not enough juice for 1 cup, add water. In heavy saucepan, mix together sugar, cornstarch, and salt. Stir in peach juice. Bring to a boil. Add butter. Cook, stirring 10 minutes. Stir in drained peaches and evaporated milk. Cook, continuing to stir 1 minute more. Pour over snowball puddings. Serves 6.

PERSIMMON PUDDING

Persimmons grow wild on trees and are said to be a favorite food of the opposum and hog. They are sweet and delicious when ripe, but bite into a green one and your mouth will stay puckered for a week.

1½ cups persimmon pulp
2 eggs
1 cup sugar
½ tsp. salt
¼ tsp. baking soda
1½ cups buttermilk
1¼ cups self-rising flour
2 tbsp. melted butter

To get pulp, rub persimmons through a colander to remove seeds and skins. Beat eggs. Add sugar, salt, and persimmon. Stir baking soda into buttermilk. Add to persimmon. Stir in flour and melted butter. Grease and flour 9-by-9-inch square baking pan. Pour mixture in. Bake in 350-degree oven for 25 to 30 minutes. Knife inserted in center should come out clean when done. Serves 8.

BRAN MUFFINS

1 tbsp. cocoa powder
1 cup bran buds
1 cup self-rising flour
⅔ cup sugar
¾ cup milk
1 egg, beaten
¼ cup butter or margarine, melted
½ tsp. vanilla

Mix together first 4 ingredients. Add milk, beaten egg, butter, and vanilla. Mix well. Spray muffin pans with cooking spray and dust with flour. Fill ⅔ full. Bake in 350-degree oven for 15 to 20 minutes, or until pick inserted in center of muffins comes out clean. Serve hot with butter. Makes 12 muffins.

FUDGE-TOPPED BROWNIES

½ cup butter or margarine
4 tbsp. cocoa powder
1 cup sugar
2 eggs, well beaten
1 cup self-rising flour
½ cup chopped nuts
½ tsp. vanilla

Melt butter. Stir in cocoa and sugar. Add well-beaten eggs. Mix in flour, nuts, and vanilla. Spread in greased 9-inch square pan. Bake in 350-degree oven for 25 to 30 minutes, or until wooden pick inserted in center comes out clean. Ice when cooled. Makes 16 2-inch squares.

ICING
¼ cup butter or margarine
2 tbsp. cocoa powder
3½ tbsp. milk
2 cups sifted confectioners' sugar
½ tsp. vanilla

Melt butter in saucepan with cocoa and milk. Remove from heat. Add sugar and vanilla. Beat until smooth. Spread on top of brownies.

ELEPHANT EARS

1 pkg. dry yeast
¼ cup warm water
2 cups all-purpose flour
2 tbsp. sugar
½ tsp. salt
1 cup butter or margarine
½ cup milk, scalded
1 egg yolk, beaten
2 tbsp. butter or margarine,
    melted
1 cup sugar
1 tsp. cinnamon
¼ cup butter or margarine, melted
½ cup chopped pecans

Dissolve yeast in warm water. Combine flour, 2 tbsp. sugar, and salt in large mixing bowl. With pastry blender, cut the 1 cup butter into flour. Combine cooled milk, yeast mixture, and beaten egg yolk. Add to flour mixture. Turn out onto floured surface and knead until smooth. Cover and let rest about 15 minutes.

Roll dough into about an 18-by-10-inch rectangle. Brush with melted butter. Combine 1 cup sugar and the cinnamon. Sprinkle ⅔ cup of the sugar-cinnamon mixture on dough. Roll up jelly roll fashion, beginning with long side. Place seam side down. Cut into 1-inch slices.

On lightly floured surface, roll each slice out to ⅛ inch thick. With spatula, carefully lift slices onto lightly greased baking sheet. Using the ¼ cup butter, spread each slice with melted butter. Sprinkle with remaining sugar-cinnamon mixture and chopped pecans. Bake in 400-degree oven for 10 minutes, or until lightly browned. Makes 18.

STRAWBERRY SHORTCAKE BISCUITS

2 cups self-rising flour
¼ tsp. baking soda
⅓ cup sugar
⅓ cup butter or margarine
⅔ cup buttermilk
Fresh sweetened strawberries
Whipped cream

Mix together flour, baking soda, and sugar. Cut in butter with pastry blender. Add buttermilk. Turn dough out onto lightly floured board. Roll to about ¼ inch thick. Cut in circles ¼ inch thick with biscuit cutter, or if larger circles are desired, cut around saucer or large-mouthed cup or glass. Place on buttered baking pan. Bake at 425 degrees 10 to 15 minutes. Split and fill with strawberries. Top with whipped cream. Makes 10 biscuits.

CHOCOLATE GRAVY

Chocolate gravy is always served for breakfast at my friend Nell's when her children and grandchildren come home.

3 tbsp. cocoa powder
1 cup sugar
2 tbsp. flour
2 cups milk

Mix cocoa, sugar, and flour in skillet. Stir in milk. Cook on medium heat, stirring until mixture thickens, about 8 minutes. Serve hot over buttered biscuits. Serves 8 to 10.

SO'GHUM 'LASSES
(Papa's Favorite Dessert)

When I was growing up in Tennessee, every community had a sorghum mill operating in the fall. It was not a very pleasant place. The huge cooker and the steam rising from the simmering molasses made the surrounding area hot, and bees swarmed around everywhere trying to get a taste of the sweet sorghum. The poor old mule went round and round in a circle pulling the grinder to crush the sorghum cane.

Papa was particular about his sorghum molasses. He would go to the mill and watch the molasses cooking in the long vat, for you see he could tell by the color and the consistency when it was just right. When it looked to suit him, he'd say, "All right, boys, dip me up 'bout five gallon now, and don't get no bees in it." Papa was a true sorghum lover. He finished off his breakfast every morning, and often other meals as well, with sorghum molasses.

1 hunk butter about the size of an
   egg
⅓ cup sorghum molasses
1 biscuit

Papa would put the butter in his plate and pour the sorghum over it. With a fork he mashed the butter up and mixed it in with the sorghum. With his knife he would pile it onto a biscuit a bite at a time and end up sopping up the last of it. One of the most pleasant memories I have of Papa is watching him enjoy his "so'ghum 'lasses."

MAMA'S ICE CREAM

Making ice cream was a new experience for the young church group my sister was entertaining. At first everyone wanted a turn at the crank; however, it soon became a chore, and one boy asked how they would know when it was done. Johnnie said, "Just keep turning until you can't turn it anymore." The boy said, "What? The crank or my arm?"

Mama used only milk, sugar, eggs, and vanilla when she made ice cream. Since we milked Jersey cows, and their milk contained such a high percentage of cream, it was not necessary to add cream. If you are making this recipe with store-bought milk, you may want to add a half-pint of whipping cream after the milk-egg mixture has cooled.

1-gal. ice-cream freezer
6 eggs
2 cups sugar
1 qt. milk, plus enough additional milk to fill freezer bucket to ⅔ full
2 tsp. vanilla
Ice
Salt

Beat eggs thoroughly. Add sugar and beat well. Stir in 1 qt. milk. Put on stove and heat, stirring often until mixture begins to smoke. Do not boil. Remove from heat. Let cool. Add vanilla. Pour into freezer bucket. Add enough milk to fill bucket ⅔ full. Stir to blend. Pack ice and salt around and turn crank until crank or your arm will no longer turn, whichever comes first. Makes 1 gallon.

MAMA'S JELLY ROLL

Although Mama "put up" several different kinds of jellies each year, she bought Rex imitation jelly for her jelly roll. It came in a tin bucket and had a very unusual flavor. I've never tasted any other like it, and have not seen it in the grocery stores in many years.

> **1 cup cake flour**
> **1 tsp. baking powder**
> **¼ tsp. salt**
> **5 eggs**
> **1 cup sugar**
> **1 tsp. vanilla**
> **Confectioners' sugar**
> **1 cup jelly, your choice**

Sift together the flour, baking powder, and salt. Set aside. Beat eggs. Gradually add sugar, beating well. Stir in flour and vanilla. Beat until smooth. Grease a 15-by-10-inch jelly roll pan. Line with waxed paper. Grease paper. Pour mixture into prepared pan. Bake in 400-degree oven for 13 minutes, or until brown. Turn out on cloth sprinkled with confectioners' sugar. Peel off paper and cut crisp edges off dough. Spread dough with jelly. Roll quickly. Wrap in cloth. Cool. Slice and serve when cooled. Serves 10.

Miscellaneous and How-To

The old setting hen. Drawing by Willie Ledford.

APPLESAUCE

4 tart apples
¼ cup water
¼ cup sugar

Peel, core, and chop apples. Cook in water in covered saucepan over medium heat until very tender, about 10 minutes. Remove from heat. Mash until smooth. Add sugar. Return to heat just until sugar dissolves, 3 to 5 minutes, stirring constantly. Makes ½ pint.

CORN RELISH

½ cup white vinegar
¼ cup sugar
½ tsp. salt
½ tsp. celery seed
¼ tsp. mustard seed
1 can (12 oz.) whole-kernel corn,
  with red and green peppers
½ cup chopped celery
½ cup chopped green onion

In saucepan, mix together vinegar, sugar, salt, celery seed, and mustard seed. Bring to a boil for about 2 minutes. Remove from heat. Stir in drained corn, celery, and green onions. Chill before serving. Makes 1½ pints.

GREEN TOMATO RELISH

1 gal. green tomatoes
12 onions
12 green peppers
12 red peppers
½ cup salt
3 qt. vinegar
5 cups sugar
1 tbsp. tumeric
2 tbsp. mixed pickling spices, tied
    into a cheesecloth bag

Wash and cut off stem end of tomatoes, but do not peel. Cut into quarters. Peel and quarter onions. Cut off stem end and seed peppers. Cut into quarters. Put coarse-grind blade in food mill. Grind all vegetables. Add salt to vegetables, mixing thoroughly. Let set overnight.

To vinegar add sugar, tumeric, and pickling spices. Bring to boil. Turn down to simmer and cook 20 minutes. Add tomato mixture. Let come to a boil. Remove from heat. Pack into sterilized jars and seal. Makes about 8 pints.

PICKLED PIG'S FEET

Remove toes and claws from feet. Scrape off all hair and clean feet thoroughly. Cook in large pot with enough water to cover. Simmer several hours until tender. Drain, rinse clean, and chill feet. Pack in jars. Split 2 red cayenne pepper pods. Add to each jar. Pour white vinegar to within ½ inch of top. Seal. Store in refrigerator or cool place. Will keep 3 to 5 weeks.

PICKLED BEETS

4 lb. beets
Boiling water
2 cups sugar
2 cups water
2 cups vinegar
2 tbsp. mixed pickling spices

Wash beets, leaving on roots and 1 inch of tops. If cut, beets will bleed. Cook covered in boiling water for 25 minutes. Drain. Slip off skins. Trim and cut beets into quarters. In large pot, mix sugar, 2 cups water, and vinegar. Tie spices in cheesecloth bag. Add to pot. Bring to a boil. Add beets. Simmer 10 minutes. Pack beets and liquid into hot half-pint jars, leaving ½ inch headspace. Process by placing in hot water bath for 30 minutes. Start timing when water begins to boil. Makes 6 to 7 half-pints.

PICKLED OKRA

3 lb. okra, pods 2 to 3 inches
   long
6 red hot peppers
6 cloves garlic, peeled
2 tbsp. celery seed
2 tbsp. mustard seed
2 tbsp. dillseed
2 cups white vinegar
2 cups water
4 tbsp. salt
2 tbsp. sugar

Wash okra, peppers, and garlic. Place 1 pepper, 1 garlic clove, and 1 tsp. each of celery, mustard, and dillseed in each of 6 sterilized pint jars. Pack okra tightly into jars. Mix together in saucepan vinegar, water, salt, and sugar. Let come to a boil until sugar is dissolved. Pour boiling mixture over okra to within ¼ inch of top. Seal jars and process in hot water bath for 10 minutes.

PORK SAUSAGE

6 lb. ground pork
2 tbsp. ground sage
5 tsp. salt
2 tsp. black pepper
1 tsp. red cayenne pepper

Mix all ingredients together, using hands. Make into patties. Put wax paper between patties to keep from sticking together. Wrap in freezer paper. Freeze till ready to eat, then fry. Makes about 48 patties.

BEEF JERKY

1 lb. beef round steak
Salt and pepper

Remove all fat from steak and partly freeze. Bias-slice the partially frozen steak into very thin strips. Place a single layer of strips in a bowl. Sprinkle generously with salt and pepper. Repeat layering till all meat is used, salting and peppering each layer. Weigh meat down with heavy object. Cover and chill overnight.

Drain meat. Pat dry with paper towels. Arrange a single layer of meat strips on a rack in shallow baking pan. Bake in 300-degree oven for about 45 minutes. Cool, then store in airtight container in refrigerator.

MUSCADINE JAM

Muscadines are wild grapes that grow in abundance in the woods and hills of Tennessee. They are almost as large as domestic grapes and are very tasty. They also make excellent jam and jelly.

Muscadines
Water to cover
4 cups sugar

Wash muscadines. Place in large pan and cover with water. Let come to a boil. Boil about 15 minutes. Put through a colander, mashing to push the pulp through. Discard seeds and peels. Measure out 6 cups, or measure and add 4 cups sugar for every 6 cups of muscadines.

Place on stove. Bring to a boil. Turn heat to medium. Cook, stirring occasionally, about 30 minutes. Test by putting a tablespoonful of mixture on saucer that has been in freezer. If mixture does not readily run, the jam is done. Pour into jars and seal. Makes 3 pints.

PEPPER JELLY

This is a good accompaniment to ham or most any meat. It is also good with beans and greens.

6 medium peppers, red or green
2 large hot peppers
6 cups sugar
1 cup white vinegar
½ cup water
1 bottle (6 oz.) liquid fruit pectin
Red or green food coloring
**   (optional)**

Put peppers through coarse grind of food chopper. Place in colander and press out juice. Strain juice through cheesecloth. Hopefully you will have 1⅔ cups juice. If not, add water. Place juice in large saucepan. Add sugar, vinegar, and water. Bring to a boil. Add pectin. Boil rapidly for 1 minute. Remove from heat. Add few drops red or green food coloring, if desired. Skim off foam. Pour into hot jars and seal. Fills 4 half-pint jars.

WATERMELON RIND PRESERVES

6 cups white part of watermelon,
   cut into 1-inch squares
4 cups water
¼ cup coarse salt
2 cups sugar
1 cup white vinegar
1 cup water
1 tbsp. broken cinnamon stick
1 tsp. whole cloves
½ lemon, thinly sliced

In large kettle, mix watermelon, 4 cups water, and salt. Let stand overnight. Drain and rinse. Cover with cold water. Cover pot and cook until tender, about 25 minutes. Drain and set aside. In saucepan, mix sugar, vinegar, 1 cup water, and spices. Simmer 10 minutes. Strain.

Add lemon and watermelon. Simmer uncovered about 25 minutes, until watermelon looks clear. Remove lemon. Pack watermelon and syrup into hot half-pint jars, leaving ½-inch headspace. Seal and process in boiling water bath for 5 minutes. Fills 6 half-pint jars.

STRAWBERRY PRESERVES

6 cups crushed strawberries
4½ cups sugar

Combine strawberries and sugar. Let stand in refrigerator over-night. Place in large Dutch oven. Let come to a boil. Boil 15 to 20 minutes, stirring occasionally to prevent sticking, until mixture has thickened. Remove from heat. Skim off any foam. Pour into hot jars. Seal and process in boiling water bath for 5 minutes. Makes 4 half-pints.

LEATHER BREECHES
(Dried Green Beans)

Kentucky wonder beans are the best to raise if you want to dry them. Using a large needle and heavy string, string beans. Hang in dry place such as an attic or smokehouse. When dried, remove as many beans as needed to fill a large Dutch oven. Cover with water to soak overnight.

Add 1 teaspoon baking soda to beans and let come to a boil. Turn heat to low, cover pot and cook 1 hour, adding more water if needed. Drain and wash beans. Add more water and H pound chopped salt pork. Cook 2 more hours, adding more water if needed, or until beans are soft and done. Add salt to taste.

SAUERKRAUT

Mama made kraut the old-fashioned way, by salting it down in a churn with a weight on top to keep it submerged in the brine. This is her recipe. A recipe follows for a much simpler method that works just as well.

10 heads cabbage
½ cup coarse salt

Quarter cabbages. Remove stalks and tough outer leaves. Chop or shred cabbages as thin as possible. Place in large dishpan. Mix in salt with hands. Let set about 30 minutes. Pack into churn. Press down until juice rises and covers cabbage. Weigh down with dinner plate and a clean nonelectric iron. Cover top of churn with cheesecloth. Let ferment for 5 weeks. Drain and pack in jars. Process in hot water bath for 15 minutes. Makes about 16 quarts.

EASY SAUERKRAUT

Chopped cabbage
1 cup salt
1 cup white vinegar
1 gal. water

Chop cabbage or shred as fine as possible. May use food processor. Dissolve salt and vinegar in water. Pack cabbage in sterilized jars, leaving 2 inches headspace. Pour water mixture over cabbage. Seal and keep in dark place. Ready to eat in 4 weeks.

SOUCE
(Hog's Head Cheese)

Thoroughly clean all parts of the hog head to be used. Place in large kettle with enough water to cover. Cook until meat can easily be separated from bones, about 1H hours. Strain liquid and chop meat fine. Return meat to kettle. Season with salt, red pepper flakes, and sage to taste. Cover with the strained liquid. Boil about 15 minutes longer. Pour mixture into shallow pan. Cover with cheesecloth and weigh down. When cold, mixture will slice and make delicious sandwiches or you can serve with crackers.

TARTAR SAUCE

4 cups mayonnaise
½ cup sweet pickle relish
½ cup sour chowchow
1 cup chopped green onions
1 cup chopped parsley
1 tsp. hot sauce
1 tsp. Worcestershire sauce

Mix all ingredients together. Serve with fish. Makes 1 quart.

HOW TO CLEAN AND PLUCK
A CHICKEN

This section and the following one on How to Kill a Hog may sound a bit barbaric. However, I thought it was important, not only for those who would use these methods, but for our younger generation to know the unpleasantness we had to endure "in the olden days" in order to enjoy the deliciousness of fried chicken and country ham.

Have a large pot of water boiling. Wring chicken's neck (pick a grassy spot so the chicken won't get so dirty). To wring neck, get a firm grip on the chicken's neck right behind the head. Swing it around with a quick jerk. The jerk and the weight of the chicken will pop its head right off. You'll wind up with the head in your hand and the chicken flopping on the ground. After it quits flopping, proceed with the plucking.

To make feathers easier to pluck, hold chicken by its feet and douse in boiling water for about 5 minutes. Pick all feathers off, being sure to get all small pin feathers. If you don't have long fingernails, use a paring knife to pull them out. Singe hairs off chicken by holding it by the feet and neck over a fire and turning it from side to side. We always took it outside and burned a newspaper. Be careful not to burn yourself. Don't hold it over the fire too long. It only takes a second to burn the hair off and you don't want to blacken the skin. If you do, just wash and scrape with knife.

Now you are ready to cut up the chicken. Cut the feet off where they join the legs. Discard. Cut off wings where joined at the shoulders. Cut off legs where joined to the back. Cut where legs bend to make a thigh and a drumstick. Wash these pieces and put into large pan.

There are 2 slender bones going from the shoulders down the back on both sides. You can feel these right under the skin. Start at the back and slit these up to the shoulders. Hold neck with one hand, the breast bones where the slits end with the other hand, and pull chicken apart. Cut apart below breast. Cut down at the top of breast bone, then cut slanting up. This will cut out the pully bone, or wishbone as some call it. Cut breast in half. Wash and throw pieces in pan.

Next cut around tail hole where innards join the back. Pull out innards. Pull out lungs and kidneys attached to inner back. Discard. Cut off neck. Cut back about ⅓ down from neck. This makes the saddle piece and the back. Wash and put in pan with other pieces.

Cut away the liver from the innards, being careful not to burst the gall bladder, which is attached to the liver. It is green and contains a very bitter liquid. If this gets on the liver, it won't be fit to eat. Cut out the gizzard. Cut gash in the thickest part of the gizzard, but do not cut through the inner lining. This is the gravel sack. Remove sack and discard. Wash liver and gizzard and put in pan with other pieces. Discard all other innards. The liver, gizzard, and neck are called giblets, and are very good eating. Some people save the heart, but I've heard it said if a chicken has any kind of disease, it will settle in the heart, so I throw it away.

Add 2 teaspoons salt to the pan with chicken parts. Cover with water, stirring around to dissolve the salt. If frying, just drain chicken and dredge in self-rising flour. You won't have to add more salt.

HOW TO KILL A HOG

The hog killing should occur at a time when the temperature will remain 35 degrees or under for at least two weeks. If the temperature where meat is being cured gets above 40 degrees and stays there for very long, the meat may spoil before it takes the cure. Start at daybreak, for it will take all day to finish the job of killing a hog and getting it prepared to begin the cure the following day.

Make a fire under a big wash kettle. Fill it with water. Papa used a large vat big enough for a hog to fit into. It was made of heavy metal and looked much like a huge, deep bread pan. A hole was dug. Hot coals from the fire were spread into the hole. The vat sat on top of the coals. Boiling water from the kettle was put into the vat. The coals kept the water hot.

For the kill, a .22 rifle bullet between the eyes will kill the hog instantly. After this, stick a sharp knife in the jugular vein located under the neck. Allow time for it to bleed. Put the hog on a wooden skid and drag it to the vat. It will take 3 or 4 men to handle a big hog. Lower the hog into the vat. Leave it in hot water until the hair will slip off with the bare hand. Put it back on the skid and scrape with a sharp knife.

Prepare to hang the hog. Cut a grappling stick from a large limb or from a 2 x 4. Sharpen the grappling stick on both ends. Insert the stick through tendons behind the two back hooves of the hog. Hang the hog from a big tree limb or scaffold. Place a tub under the hog to catch the entrails. Cut all the way down the middle of the belly. The entrails will fall out into the tub. No part of the hog has to be wasted. Even the intestines can be cleaned and eaten. They are called chitter-lings.

After gutting the hog, cut up, wash and dry meat. Let cool over-night. Papa cured his meat for a long time using only salt. This is his salt-cure method: Rub meat with coarse salt, being careful to rub in good around the bones. Place a layer of salt in a large wooden crate. Lay meat on top. Cover with more salt. After two weeks, brush off salt. Hang from the rafters of the smokehouse.

The meat was good cured this way, but I thought it much better when he started using sugar-cure. Papa never smoked his meat. He said it was too much trouble, and he didn't like it as well, anyhow. I've never tasted any meat bought at the grocery that comes close to the delicious taste of home-cured when using Papa's sugar-cure recipe.

SUGAR CURE FOR PORK

6 lb. salt
4 oz. saltpeter
2 lb. brown sugar
3 oz. red pepper
3 oz. black pepper

Flatten cardboard boxes and lay on large table. Mix all ingredients together. Rub meat morning and night for 3 days. Be sure to rub in good around bones. After first rub, lay meat skin-side up. Turn after each rub. The 4th day put strong wire through shank of hams and shoulders, and at corners of middlings (sides). Hang from rafters of smokehouse or shed. Place pan or papers underneath. As it takes the cure it will continue to drip. Meat may become molded after hanging several weeks. This doesn't mean it is spoiled. Just trim off mold when ready to cook. This is enough mixture to cure a good-sized hog.

HOW TO FRY CHITTERLINGS

This announcement appeared recently in the society section of our small town weekly:

Billy and Sue, Bobby and Peggy Marvin, Brown Ward and wife all had a chitterling supper at the home of Mr. and Mrs. Elbert Marvin last week and all enjoyed the feast.

Chitterlings are the large intestines of a hog. At hog-killing time, nothing was wasted when I was a child. Mama and Aunt Ibbie cleaned the foul-smelling things by running their hands down them to remove the waste. They were then split open, washed several times, put into the wash kettle outside to boil, then washed again.

True chitterling lovers will assure you that if you ever try one you'll be hooked. They look delicious fried up all nice and brown, but I could never bring myself to eat one, remembering from whence they come. Chitterlings are sold in most Southern grocery stores today. Even with U.S.D.A. approval, they still don't smell so good.

Cover chitterlings with water. Boil about 1 hour until tender. Make batter of 1 beaten egg and 1 cup milk mixed together. Sprinkle chitterlings with salt. Dip in batter, then in self-rising flour. Fry in deep hot fat until brown.

HOW TO BOIL A COUNTRY HAM

Mama used her big oval copper kettle for boiling ham. If you don't have a copper kettle (and who does these days?), a large enamel water bath canner or a lard can may be used. Mama's copper kettle is gone forever. If I allowed myself to think of how careless we were to lose such a treasure, I think I would go out of my mind.

Wash ham and trim off any mold. Place in kettle and cover with water. Bring to a boil. Cover kettle and boil gently 20 minutes for each pound of ham. Remove from heat and let cool in broth. Remove from broth and cut away skin. Sprinkle generously with black pepper. Slice to serve.

MAMA'S CHICKEN PRODUCTION

As I began to recollect the wondrous platters of fried chicken often prepared at our house, I thought it only proper to tell how Mama raised her chickens.

Chicken was an easy source of meat and eggs in the olden days, but chicken production has changed so drastically. Mama not only depended on the setting of her hens for fryers and layers, but also ordered 100 baby chicks from a hatchery in Illinois three different times during the summer so as to have frying-sized chickens available all summer long. There were many get-togethers that would require many platters of fried chicken, the staple food for revival preachers and company in general.

The mailman brought the boxes of chirping chickens, all fuzzy and yellow. Revivals being a big thing after the crop was laid by, many Sundays we would clean and dress as many as six fryers and cook them before going to church. We never knew how many people would come home with us for dinner. The welcome mat was always out at our house, and with Mama being a good cook, many people took advantage of it.

After checking the encyclopedia, it really does seem a mystery to me which came first: the chicken or the egg. The house for baby chicks was about 9 by 9 feet. With no brooders or heat lamps the baby chicks were kept warm by oil lanterns hanging from the ceiling. Chicken wire surrounded the house, and after the chicks were a few weeks old they were let out into the yard during the day. Another house was for the older chickens to roost. Poles were put together much like bleachers. The chickens went into this house automatically every night, hopped upon the poles, and stayed there all night. The door was always shut to keep out foxes and other predators. There was also a laying room attached to the roosting house. Nests filled with straw surrounded the walls. When the hens began to show maternal signs, Mama would take a pencil and mark the eggs around and around so as to tell which ones to leave in the nest. Otherwise fresh eggs laid each day would get mixed in with the setting eggs and would not hatch at the proper time.

I liked gathering eggs, except in the spring when the hens were setting. We had to raise them up and check to see if there were any fresh eggs. The old setting hens seemed to be mad all the time, and if you didn't wear gloves they would peck a blood blister on your hand.

Mama's method of raising chickens seemed real modern in those days, and in our area many people still raise them in the same manner. Electric brooders and heat lamps may have taken the place of the oil lanterns, but nothing can replace the old setting hen.

HOW TO PLUCK A LIVE GOOSE

Although we did eat the eggs, Mama raised geese mostly for the down they provided for making pillows and feather beds.

Place goose on your lap with the head between your legs. Hold feet with one hand while plucking the down from the breast of the goose with the other. This is done in the spring when they begin to lose some of their feathers for the summer heat. The feathers are loose then and it doesn't hurt the goose at all. Place feathers in flour sack and hang in dry place until you have enough to make a pillow or feather bed.

HOW TO CATCH AND COOK
FROG LEGS

All that's needed to catch frogs is a flashlight, a tow sack, and a rowboat. Paddle along the riverbank as quiet as possible. When the light is shined on the frog, he will not jump and can be picked up with your hands. Put in the tow sack and hold shut until you catch another one.

Skin the legs of killed frogs and cut off feet. Soak in salt water at least 1 hour. Slash legs in several places to cut the leaders or they will jump while cooking. Rinse and sprinkle with salt. Dredge in self-rising flour and brown in hot oil. Delicious.

HOW TO COOK A COON

Clean coon, being careful to save the hide, as coonskin is a valuable fur. Place in large pot. Cover with water. Add 1 teaspoon soda. Boil for 30 minutes. Remove from heat. Drain off water and rinse off coon and pot. Return to pot. Cover with fresh water, adding 2 pods of hot pepper and 1 teaspoon salt. Let come to a boil. Cover pot and simmer until tender, about 1 hour, depending on how big the coon is. Remove from water. Place in roasting pan. Place cooked sweet potatoes around coon. Lay strips of bacon on top of coon. Make sauce.

SAUCE FOR COON

½ cup vinegar
1 tbsp. butter or margarine,
  melted
½ tsp. red pepper
½ tsp. black pepper
1 tbsp. lemon juice

Mix all together. Pour over coon and sweet potatoes. Bake 1 hour in 350-degree oven, basting often. Serves 6.

HOW TO SKIN A RABBIT

Cut off the forefeet at first joint. Cut skin around the first joint of hind leg. Loosen it, and with a sharp knife, slit the skin on underside of the leg at the tail. Pull skin and turn back until it is removed from hind legs. Tie legs together and hang from a nail on a tree. Pull the skin up over the back to the head, slipping skin off front legs as you go. Cut off head, thus removing all the hide.

Slit down the front and remove entrails. Discard. Wash inside and out. Cut up into serving pieces, cutting at the leg joints and the middle of the back. Cover with water and add ½ cup vinegar. Soak in this solution at least 2 hours or overnight. Drain and rinse again before frying. This method also applies to squirrels.

To save hide, stretch fur-side down on board. Cover with coarse salt and put in cold place where temperature reaches no more than 40 degrees. If you want to save the hind legs for good luck charms, salt them down also. They should be cured in about 2 weeks. Remove from salt and brush.

HOW TO MAKE INEXPENSIVE
CHRISTMAS TREE ORNAMENTS

Our Christmas tree was always a cedar since they grew in abundance in our part of Tennessee. We could never afford store-bought ornaments. Ropes to go around the tree were made from popcorn and red berries, using a needle and Mama's sewing thread to string them together.

We had no cookie cutters. Mama made patterns of angels, wreaths, and candy canes from cardboard, laying the patterns on the dough and cutting around them with a knife. Since we had no food coloring, we used crayons to decorate the ornaments. They will last several years if the mice don't get into them.

> **1½ cups flour**
> **1½ cups salt**
> **½ cup water, plus enough to make**
>   **claylike dough**
> **Food coloring**

Mix flour and salt together. Stir in the ½ cup water. Continue adding water a spoonful at a time until dough is like firm clay. Divide and add different colors of food coloring. Roll out on waxed paper to ½ inch thick. Cut with Christmas cookie cutters.

Make a hole in each one before baking for hanging. Bake on ungreased cookie sheets in 350-degree oven for 1 hour. These will be very hard, so don't forget to make the hole for hanging before they are baked. They can be painted after they cool if desired. Makes 8 to 10 ornaments.

HOW TO MAKE
SELF-RISING FLOUR

4 cups plain flour
2 tsp. salt
2 tbsp. baking powder

Sift together twice. Use in any recipe calling for self-rising flour.

GRANDMA LOCK'S LYE SOAP

Grandma made the lye she used for soap from wood ashes. The ashes were saved all winter in an ash hopper, a tall, square wooden box with a hole in the bottom and a tin top to keep out the rain. Come spring, rain water was poured into the top of the hopper. As the water seeped down through the ashes and ran out of the hole, it became the lye for soap making. This is a revised version of Grandma's recipe, using store-bought lye.

4 cans lye
8 gal. rain water
16 lb. grease

Mix all together in iron kettle. Boil 1 hour, stirring occasionally. Pull fire away from kettle and cover kettle. Let soap harden overnight (12 hours or more). With sharp butcher knife cut into chunks. Put in flour sack. Tie with string and hang in smokehouse.

Index